Tex Smith's

HOW TO BUILD

FIBERGLASS

HOT RODS, CUSTOMS & KIT CARS

BY LEROI TEX SMITH

Printed and bound in the United States of America

HOW TO BUILD FIBERGLASS HOT RODS, CUSTOMS & KIT CARS
FIRST PRINTED IN 1995 BY CO-PUBLISHERS:

CarTech, Inc., 11481 Kost Dam Road, North Branch, MN 55056
and
Tex Smith Publishing Company, P.O. Box 726, Driggs, ID 83422

COPYRIGHT BY LeRoi Tex Smith 1995

CarTech, Inc. and Tex Smith Publishing Company recommend you follow all safety procedures when working on your vehicle. Wear eye protection and respiration filter, especially when painting and around tools. Always dispose of hazardous fluids, batteries, tires and parts properly and safely to protect our environment.

CarTech, Inc., and Tex Smith Publishing Company books are also available at discounts in bulk quantity for industrial or sales / promotional use. For details, contact the marketing director at:
CarTech, Inc., 11481 Kost Dam Road, North Branch, MN 55056
Telephone (612) 583-3471, FAX (612) 583-2023
Tex Smith Publishing Company, P.O. Box 726, Driggs, ID 83422
Telephone (208) 354-8133, FAX (208) 354-8137

OVERSEAS DISTRIBUTION BY:

BROOKLANDS BOOKS LTD.
P.O. Box 146, Cobham, Surrey, KT11 1LG, England
Telephone 0932 865051, FAX 0932 868803

BROOKLANDS BOOKS LTD.
1/81 Darley Street, P.O. Box 199, Mona Vale, NSW 2103, Australia
Telephone 2 997 8428, FAX 2 452 4679

ISBN 1-884089-10-0

Printed and bound in the United States of America.

AUTHOR	LeRoi Tex Smith
PUBLISHER	LeRoi Tex Smith
EDITOR	Brian Brennan
TECHNICAL EDITOR	Ron Ceridono
ART DIRECTOR	Greg Compton
ART ASSISTANT	Lisa Hanks

CONTENTS

FOREWORD

This book is about the use of fiberglass and related products by the specialty car builder. It is not an engineering treatise, but it is of value for the professional and ideal for the home builder.

Fiberglass, and its associates in every guise, has changed the world. Beginning with an accident in a chemical lab, 'glass has become the building material of choice for an industry that reaches into every facet of human existence. For the automotive enthusiast, it can be a most important product of participation in the hobby / sport. In short, for the car person, fiberglass is wonderful.

I learned about fiberglass during the 1940s, when it was being touted as the wonder material of all time. I had learned the basics of metal fabrication from some California "old world" craftsmen, but at that time local fiberglass experiments were limited primarily to boat builders and a few aircraft pioneers. By the early Fifties, however, fiberglass was gaining widespread use in Southern California and there was an entire specialty automotive industry emerging because of it.

Limited-production vehicle manufacturers have always been able to create and make workable chassis, with parts readily available through supplier pipelines. In the earlier days of American vehicle manufacturing, a new mass production builder could purchase everything from frames to rolling chassis to full power-trains. They could even buy bodies from a number of coachbuilders. From the 1930s on, the problems seem to revolve around bodies. Making a metal vehicle body by hand is too costly, tooling for a production run is more costly. Fiberglass solved those problems.

Overnight, a spate of special cars was introduced to the public, nearly every one with a fiberglass body. At least in the prototype stage. Interestingly, the technology for such body construction, and much of the basic material, has changed very little during the ensuing years. At the same time, the use of fiberglass products in specialty car building, by the professional supplier and the backyard builder, has increased dramatically. Unfortunately, information on the subject has been sorely lacking.

The limited-production sports special really brought fiberglass before the public as a viable body construction process. The Glaspar, and the similar Woodill Wildfire, generated a great deal of print and movie exposure during the early 1950s. These would have been the original kit cars.

The first fiberglass Model T bodies were very basic, with the only option being either a turtle deck trunk or a pickup bed. Later, the pickup bed was shortened on production T's as the car show-oriented Fad-T became popular.

In the years following World War II, hot rods and custom cars got all the attention, but an active cadre of homebuilders was creating what were to eventually be called "sports specials." These highly modified production cars, most often on pre-1949 Ford chassis, usually had bodies so drastically changed that they didn't resemble the more common custom. Often, the cars were radically sectioned, tops were removed, and in many ways these specials were backyard sports cars. Because these homebuilts got so much attention in the general interest mechanical magazines (*Popular Mechanics,* etc.), they appealed to a much greater audience than hot rods and customs. Which is what led to the use of one-off fiberglass bodies. Amateur builders felt less intimidated by fiberglass than by the prospect of reshaping metal. This, in turn, gave rise to low-production specials in the 1950s, with names such as Glaspar, Kellison, Devin, Astra, Aztec, Woodill Wildfire, etc. And this, in turn, led to the fiberglass dune buggy craze of the Sixties and Seventies.

These first production specials were created at the time when Corvette was giving fiberglass its first major-league legitimacy as a car body material. But while the fiberglass may have been the same, the difference in production methods used for the "high" volume Corvette and the trickle of specials was a widening gulf. As a matter of record, it might be forcefully argued that those low-volume production specials of the Fifties and early Sixties (and, later, the dune buggies) were really just kit cars. Certainly, they spawned an active industry that is very separate from hot rodding and customs, and one that is generating considerable excitement of its own (especially with all the Cobra copies).

Stripped down Volkswagen sedans began to show up at Southern California sand dunes in the early 1960s, at first as bare floorplans with engines, then with tubing roll bars / cages. I was at *Hot Rod Magazine* at that time and did considerable reporting on these vehicles. One

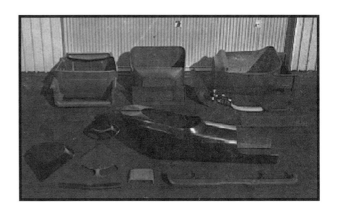

The earliest use of fiberglass in hot rodding was directed at drag racing. The Model T bodies were excellent for class racers, the dragster body was never an overwhelming favorite, but the hoods and scoops and related parts were good sellers to the stock car drag racing crowd.

One of the first turnkey hot rod kit cars was from Dragmaster, a Southern California company specializing in dragster components. The Street T featured a double-tube torsion bar suspension chassis and fiberglass body.

day, Bruce Myers called with news that he had a fiberglass body I should see. Surrounded in the Newport Beach / Balboa Island area by boat builders, fiberglass was not a new thing to Bruce. His Myers Manx fiberglass body was designed to fit an unmodified VW floorplan, which made creation of a dune buggy an

A dune buggy body on a stock VW chassis is what really introduced the general public to fiberglass as a medium for specialty cars. This vehicle could be used anywhere, it was almost indestructible, and it was inexpensive to build.

Dozens of different dune buggy bodies were produced, some strictly for racing but most were for family outings. It is now a growing trend to find and restore these charmers.

While the sports special cars were getting ever-more sophisticated in the chassis department, the specific-use chassis for dune buggies were designed for casual use at first, evolving into high-tech race chassis much later. This frame was created for use with a fiberglass body by Dearborn Motor Company in Marblehead, Massachusetts.

afternoon affair. The Manx was a sensation, and copy cats sprang up overnight nationwide. It is highly probable that only one-tenth of production buggy fiberglass bodies ever saw daylight as finished cars, but thousands and

thousands were produced. Some of those bodies were good, others were awful. It must be noted that in recent years, fiberglass-bodied dune buggies have become a target for restoration, many as show cars, and they are usually available at very low prices.

While the sports specials were appearing as low-volume items, fiberglass was used to make a few replacement and custom parts in hot rodding, primarily for drag racing cars. In the late Fifties, Bud Lang and Curt Hamilton hit on the idea of making a 1923 Ford Model T bucket body, initially as something for drag racers who wanted such a lightweight body for class racing. As with the later Manx, copies of that first 'glass T appeared immediately. Some were hand-laminated, and cheaper versions were very thin, usually made with a chopper gun. All were available, initially, as body skins only. Then, the manufacturers began adding plywood floors and wood substructures. Opening doors became options, at a price, of course. Magazines did how-to articles on such bodies, usually about adding the wood. The

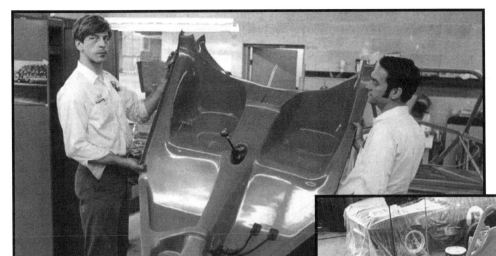

If the stock VW floorplan was used, there was no need for an inner passenger tub, but the Dearborn vehicle special frame also required a fiberglass floorplan.

The evolving dune buggy took fiberglass use to the extremes, and some of this technology transferred to sports specials, some to race cars.

fiberglass T bucket, sometimes called a Fad Car and sometimes referred to as a Modified (the name for the abbreviated T roadster at dry lakes events) was a major part of the emerging street rod hobby during the 1960s. But, for hot rodding, fiberglass remained a lesser item... until the arrival of the "big" bodies. That is, the Model A / 1932 / 1934 bodies.

These bigger bodies required much more attention than the T bucket. Dee Wescott from the Portland, Oregon, area pioneered the

Model A parts in the 1950s, and his first 1932 Ford roadster was a dramatic new product. Other Deuce bodies had been built by various entrepreneurs, sometimes as a potential commercial venture, but such cars in the Sixties were still considered "cake mix" vehicles. The phrase "steel is real" held sway. As in kit cars, the big change in hot rodder acceptance of fiberglass bodies came with the introduction of aftermarket reproduction frame and suspension components.

New frames and attendant parts meant that starting in the 1970s it was possible to build a complete "new" old car... if a fiberglass body were used. During the early Seventies, restored Model As and early V8 Fords were bringing premium

In an attempt to be different, some dune buggies were disguised as pseudo hot rods. The concept never caught on.

The major change in hot rodder use of fiberglass for street driven cars came when the larger Model A and 1932 Ford roadster and touring bodies were introduced. These bodies, along with new aftermarket frames and suspension components, created a hot rod kit car that is sometimes superior to original factory equipment.

dollars. By the late Seventies, however, it was apparent that a really well-built hot rod would bring more dollars than the same car restored. Customers appeared from everywhere, buying up all available desirable rods at major rod and custom events. At the same time, casual hot rodders who had building talents began backyard businesses, assembling cars with all new components. This turn of events was paralleled in the kit car industry, but to a lesser degree. An individual with the right skills could create a handful of cars each year, earning well above his normal wages. The fiberglass industry

began to boom, and the selection of body styles for hot rodding expanded accordingly. Non-Ford products started to appear, first with early model Chevrolet items, then with Chrysler Corporation styles. By the late Eighties, it was apparent that fiberglass car bodies for a variety of "late models" would also evolve. This has given rise to still more suppliers.

During this time of commercial applications of fiberglass bodies for specialty cars, the custom builders continued to work. Foremost among these customizers was Ed "Big Daddy" Roth. Until recent years, Roth created his fantastic concepts in Southern California, today he continues his avocation in Manti, Utah.

It is only a small step from the 1935-36 Ford to the 1937 and later bodies, at first the suppliers concentrate on body styles that are most popular, then they arrive with other styles (coupes, sedans, etc.) and sometimes even offer "phantom" bodies, or styles that were never produced by a factory. Chevrolet and MoPar bodies are also now available.

Manufacturers of hot rod bodies have continued to improve technology until it is now possible to create modern size car bodies from fiberglass. The 1935-36 Fords were the first of the "Fat" Fords to be done in 'glass.

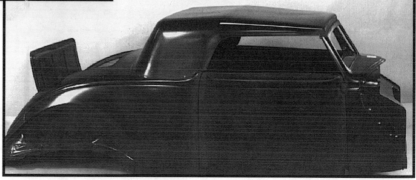

Dick Dean, a veteran race and show car builder from California, created a combination kit car special and dune buggy with his Shalako. Fiberglass is perfect for low-volume production for similar cars.

Custom car shows came on very big during the 1960s, and Ed Roth rode the popularity wave by building a variety of show vehicles, all relying on highly styled fiberglass bodies. Because fiberglass offered a chance to build some truly avant garde designs, the Roth creations captured the imagination of car enthusiasts worldwide, many of the machines appeared as miniature model kits. In a way, Roth made fiberglass a legitimate art medium, a fact verified by his several fine art museum one-man shows in recent years.

Fiberglass also became a material of choice among race car builders, from the high-banked NASCAR ovals to drags to sports car circuits. Fiberglass parts are quick to fabricate, inexpensive, and relatively lightweight. Recently, more exotic resin composites have become bread and butter components for the most high-tech racers. In the high-volume production arena, however, fiberglass has a so-so acceptance. Plastics, in general, are in greater use, but Corvette remains the only real

performer with fiberglass. For the immediate future, that seems to be the undisputed fact.

Fiberglass is good; it is something that the limited-volume manufacturer and backyard builder can use with excellent results, and it is a procedure with an excellent cost-to-product ratio. That's what this book is about… using fiberglass in specialty car building.

Harrah's Automobile Museum in Reno acquired several of Ed Roth's fiberglass-bodied show works, these vehicles are excellent examples of one-off creations where body cost can be controlled.

As the specialty fiberglass body industry has matured, more and more complex projects have been introduced to the market. Legendary customizer Gene Winfield makes this 1949-51 Mercury body; it comes complete with most of the customizing tricks already done, including a chopped top, and the body will fit over a slightly modified modern chassis.

WORKING SMART

Fiberglass looks innocent enough. Some kinda smelly watery looking stuff and some slick fabric. Nothing to it. Wrong! Fiberglass will jump up and bite you when you get careless. Amateurs get careless, professionals get careless. The way to avoid most of the problems is to know what the dangers are, use the correct tools correctly, and include safe personal work habits.

All of this starts with the work area. Because heat is a working partner to fiberglassing resins, always select a place where the "room" temperature will be relatively constant, at least through complete cure time for the resin. Working outside is acceptable, even desirable, but work in the shade and in a dirt free area when possible. Humidity is not a friend, so stay away from anything that adds lots of moisture to the air, and select times when ambient humidity is not extremely high. If working outside in temperatures below 60 degrees, it is best to move the project inside shortly after lay-up, so that curing will take place in a warmer zone.

Although working outside eliminates some of the problems of hazardous vapor build-up, and you want to work upwind of the project, the ideal place to do fiberglass work is in a well-ventilated, well-lit room with controlled temperature. Not as impossible as it may seem, since a home garage can be all these things. Ventilation should always be provided by a fan moving the air out of the work area, not in. It's a necessity, even if this costs you internal room heat during the winter. Don't direct this ventilated air toward a house.

Since fiberglass and resin are going to get most everywhere you don't want them to be, plan ahead. A concrete floor (indoors or out) can be covered with large sheets of plastic,

even paper in a squeeze. Resin loves to stick to cement, but concrete can have a sealer finish applied (something you have probably wanted to do anyway), it can have a commercial paint applied, and it can even be waxed. All of this effort pays off when it comes time to clean up the mess.

Make up a work table that can be discarded if it becomes too messy, or keep the table covered with plastic. Keep a supply of water available, but well away from the project, and keep a gallon or so of Acetone handy for instant clean-up. Make sure there is absolutely no open flame anywhere in the area, especially not an open flame heater. Avoid even a chance for a stray spark of some kind, and keep an updated fire extinguisher available. This means no smoking around fiberglass agents, either. Fiberglassing agent vapors are heavy, they sink to the floor area. Many resins are flammable, in both liquid and cured form, even the fire retardant type of resin can burn in liquid form. Some of the more exotic resins can explode, particularly if the chemicals are not mixed in proper sequence. Never store fiberglassing chemicals in the sun or near flame. Always store the materials in a cool, dry, darkened area. Do not store any chemicals in metal containers. If you read the safety instructions on these chemicals, you'll note that some of them can spontaneously combust.

While you don't normally think of clothing as a tool, it is such a thing when working with fiberglass. Passive, but part of the overall approach. When any amount of fiberglassing is to be done, it is next to impossible to keep resin and reinforcing material from building up on footwear. You can plan on donating a pair of boots to nothing but fiberglass work, or you can buy some polyethylene disposable "boots" from the paint store. They slip over shoes and boots, and are throw-away cheap. Same with polyethylene gloves, which you'll go through in quantity. Use the gloves the entire time you're working with the uncured products, wear stronger plastic gloves when sanding and trimming. Save your skin. Throw-away coveralls, which are sold to automotive painters, work very well as a shield to fiberglass chemicals and fibers, and with care they can be used a number of times before discarding. Some of these painter's coveralls also have hoods, which you'll come to appreciate quickly.

Clear goggles are imperative, for use at all times, from mixing chemicals to lay-up to finish sanding. Never let fiberglassing chemical get in your eyes, read the caution labels on all products so you know what to do in case of an eye contact accident, and don't let an accident go untreated.

Always use respirators or filter masks, even outdoors in what seems to be a perfectly fiberglass-particle-free environment. Masks do not protect against fumes, respirators do. If you are working with fiberglass in the first place, you probably also get involved with spraying automotive paints, so a respirator is a great investment. Get a good one, something that has replaceable cartridges that filter all kinds of harmful fumes. (Read the literature before buying, and don't be stingy!) Replacement lungs cost far more than good respirators.

Some of the chemicals can cause severe skin burns, most of the traditional types of glass fiber cause irritation and itching where they contact bare skin. The first line of defense is to keep these elements off the body to begin with. Secondly, use lots of talcum powder and skin lotion before starting a project, and shower very well afterward, followed by lotion if itching persists. Do not wash skin with acetone! Use a gel-type hand cleaner, followed by lots of water and soap. That's one of the reasons for having a good supply of water handy to your work area, so you can wash often.

The tools used for fiberglassing work are,

for the most part, found in every car enthusiast's garage. The real key for having these tools after the fiberglass project is finished is in keeping them cleaned. You cannot easily get rid of resin that has cured, so clean all tools immediately after use. Use acetone for polyester and special solvent for epoxy or other exotic resins.

The ordinary tools you'll use include razor blades, sandpaper, electric drill with both metal and wood bits, hacksaw and sabre saw, electric sander, air compressor, hammers, clamps, files, a spray gun, etc. Special tools will be really good scissors for cutting the fiberglass fabrics (which you should cut in a clean area away from resins), paint brushes, mixing sticks, squeegees, and a variety of mixing containers. It is usually most convenient to use disposable containers, small ones for little jobs and large pans for big jobs. Don't use a waxed paper, since the resin will usually melt the wax, and don't use styrofoam (which will also melt).

Mix resins in the mixing containers, not in the original containers. Don't reuse a mixing stick in uncatalyzed resin. Learn to mix just enough resin, because all the excess you throw away is costly.

Finally, consider cellophane your friend. You'll end up using it for a lot of tricks, because resin does not stick to it. An example of this is using cellophane over the top of a fiberglass repair. The cellophane can be smoothed very well with any suitable tool, even a paint roller, resulting in a cured finish that requires less sanding than otherwise. Cellophane also can be used on fiberglass that is in a mold, to get a smoother inner surface.

You can't get enough rags or paper towels, so keep a large supply on hand, and plan on throwing the entire lot away after use.

Finishing tools are mostly sanders and polishers that are common to a car enthusiast anyway.

MATERIALS

Let's get things straight, right off. The correct name should be Fiberglass Reinforced Plastic, as the plastics industry is wont to say. But we'll just go ahead and call it fiberglass, or simply 'glass. The resin used to make fiberglass is a plastic, the reinforcing agent is strands (fibers) of glass.

Despite its reputation as a low-cost material, fiberglass is not always the most inexpensive way to create a special car body or part. The real value is that someone with limited (or no) talent for metal work *can* do 'glass. You can also do some pretty tricky shapes with fiberglass that would be nearly impossible with metal. You can buy smaller quantities of automotive-oriented fiberglass products at most any hardware or auto parts store. However, be prepared to pay a premium when you purchase in such limited amounts. If you shop at a boat supply outlet, you may pay higher prices than you might at major discount chain stores. Most larger cities have fiberglass product suppliers. The real key is to work with *quality* fiberglass materials, your supplier should steer you to the better brands. Avoid the cheap stuff, because that's usually exactly how it works. If you are going to jump off the deep end and create your own car body, you are working in such large quantities that you should check with manufacturers and wholesale houses. Always plan your schedule in such a way that you buy your resin and 'glass at the time you need it. Resin does have a short shelf life, which is normally never more than a year, so you don't want it hanging around the garage for two years before you get around to the project. Store resin in a cool place, heat (even sunlight) will cause it to "go off," or set. You also want to keep your fiberglass cloth or matte uncontaminated with typical home

garage grunge. If you plan well ahead, and are patient, you can often take advantage of sales savings, just remember shelf life. You can also buy surplus resin and fiberglass products from major regional users (boat builders, home product builders, etc), but if you do, be sure the fiberglass is fresh, and what you want to use on a car body. There is a difference in fiberglass finishes, especially in commercial applications, and these finishes can be affected adversely by time. The point is, shop around, ask questions of the supplier, and save money, but don't buy poor quality and don't linger once you start a project.

RESINS

Resin is plastic, but it isn't the kind of plastic we normally associate with car parts. Of itself, a cured sheet of "commonly available" resin will become brittle. It needs reinforcement. But polyester resins come in different stages of flexibility, from very rigid to very flexible. The more flexible the resin, the less it will crack or craze from impact or age. There are also a number of different synthetic resins, such as the epoxies, the polyesters, the ureas, the acrylics, and the phenolics. For car bodies, and most of the parts we need, a modestly rigid polyester resin is the material of choice, since it is easy to work with, will give good stiffness, and is less expensive.

Viscosity is a measure of polyester's resistance to flowing, and polyester resins can vary from under 100 cps to around 70,000 cps. That's from thin as water to thick and sluggish. For hobby and commercial use something around 700 cps is best. At this "thickness," the polyester flows well and will thoroughly saturate (wet) fiberglass cloth and matte. If a thicker resin is needed, a thickening material (thixotropic powder) can be added. A thicker resin works well on vertical or overhead applications where the thinner resin drips or runs too readily.

Heat is what makes resin harden, or set. The polyester used for car parts and bodies can be cured (set) by internal chemical heat, external heat, or both. Internal heat is started by adding a catalyst and an accelerator. Heat causes the resin molecules to link into chains, in turn causing the resin to harden. Once hard, heat no longer effects the cured resin. Generally, resin sold over the counter already has an accelerator added (this is usually cobalt naphthenate). The catalyst is usually methyl-ethyl-ketone peroxide. The combination becomes something that will harden at ambient (room) temperature. But, over time resin that has no catalyst added will harden, which is why you must check the date on the resin container and store it in a cool place.

Learning to control this heat factor is a basic necessity for anyone who plans on doing much fiberglass work. If you did not have an accelerator, resin with catalyst added and then subjected to around 200 degrees heat for a couple hours would have a pot life (the time it remains usable) of a couple days. Add accelerator and heat and the pot life can be timed in minutes! Since the accelerator is already present in most resin, the other factors in curing time are: amount of catalyst added, work area temperature, humidity, and the mass of resin being mixed.

The resin's internal heat will be greater, and curing will be faster, in direct proportion to the amount of fiberglass mix you create. A gallon bucket will kick (cure) faster than a half-gallon, and so on. Also, the same amount of resin spread out in a large flat pan will give a longer working time, which is why it takes longer for resin spread over a part to kick.

As a general rule, you will add about two percent catalyst by weight (resin weighs about 9 pounds per gallon) to a given amount of resin. This works out to one-half percent by volume. Try and become very conscious about mixing exactly the same each batch, then all you need consider is temperature. With the two percent ratio, and working temperatures at

Working with fiberglassing materials is not difficult, but the instructions should be followed carefully, especially in mixing ratios and working temperatures. Fiberglass materials used in automotive body and parts construction / repairs have changed very little over the years.

about 70 degrees, pot life of quality resin would be slightly over one-half hour, while curing time would be roughly two hours. Now, if the room working temperature is higher than 70 degrees, pot life and curing time will be shorter, or you must reduce the amount of catalyst slightly. By the same token, if the room temperature is below 70 degrees, you will have longer curing times, or you must add a little more catalyst. The thickness of the layer of applied resin will also affect curing time, with a thicker layer kicking faster than a thin layer. A good rule of thumb is to work at room temperatures between 60 and 90 degrees. Either side of this and you start to have problems, and you will need special formula resin. Incidentally, styrene is a thinner for polyester resin, but you would only use this if spraying resin (which requires lots of precautions and special equipment), which you will probably avoid.

Although there is strength in resin alone, and the addition of some kind of reinforcement material drastically increases this strength, the strongest combination of resin and fiberglass will be less than 50 percent resin by weight. A fiberglass part that is made in a male / female pressure mold will have as little as 25 percent resin. Since the typical low-volume car body or part is not made with such a mold, but relies on an open lay-up system, the ratio will be closer to the 50 percent maximum.

The two kinds of polyester resins used most in building and repairing a fiberglass car body or part are lay-up (laminating) and finishing (surface). Laminating resin is called air-inhibited because it never fully cures in the presence of air. It stays tacky to the touch and that's exactly what you want if you are doing several layers of fiberglass cloth or resin. By remaining tacky, the layer accepts additional layers without additional work.

A finishing resin doesn't have this air-inhibiting factor, so it is what you want for the final layer coat. Wax or some other substance is added to the resin, and when this resin is spread over the laminating resin, the wax works to the surface and seals off the air. Presto, a full cure of the entire series of layers. Special wax can be added to laminating resin to get the same effect, or the area can be covered with cellophane to eliminate air. The waxy surface of finish resin can be wiped clean with acetone, or it can be sanded if additional fiberglassing is to be done. For small jobs, you can purchase a resin that works as a finish as well as initial laminating, the two-step approach works best for something big like a body or a fender.

When a fiberglass part is made in a female mold, the initial surface of resin on the mold is the gel coat. Sometimes color is added to this gel coat, but this color finish is seldom the maximum quality that most car enthusiasts demand, and the smoothness of a fiberglass finish is not show quality, so always plan on finishing and painting any fiberglass car part as you would an ordinary metal surface. If you are trying to repair something that has a gel coat finish, you can buy gel coat repair kits. This might be of interest if you are restoring a dune buggy, since many of the buggy bodies had a colored gel coat finish (it was supposed to hold up to rough usage better than ordinary paint), but over time even a gel coat color will fade. With the new two- and three-part paint systems, a finish far superior to a gel color is possible, and these finishes are very rugged.

Epoxy resin can be used in construction and repair of fiberglass objects (it works with all the normal reinforcing materials), but for the car builder its greatest feature is the ability to make a superior bond to wood, glass, and metal. It works like a glue. Where bonding strength is vital, the first coat of resin can be epoxy, after that layer has cured, polyester resin can continue the work. Epoxy is more expensive than polyester resin, it can spontaneously combust when improperly stored, it is tough on exposed skin, and it requires greater heat and a longer time to cure. Mixing ratios of epoxy will depend on the brand, so read and follow all instructions carefully. Room temperature needs to be higher for best results with epoxy, but curing time can be drastically reduced by use of heat lamps. You can use a curing agent that will cause an epoxy resin to be flexible, and it can be thinned without loss of strength.

There are some special pre-pregnated epoxy sheets that commercial users find useful, for the most part these are impractical for the homebuilder. One group of epoxies, however, that race car builders like, cures at room temperature. These cure very strong, and have an in-use temperature maximum nearing 450 degrees. Trade names include Ren and Hysol.

For a typical fiberglass car project, the amount of epoxy resin utilized will be far and away less than the polyester resin. If possible, epoxy should be purchased on an as-needed basis. Epoxy resin costs about six times the price of polyester resin.

VINYL ESTERS

Not as well known in the car hobby are vinyl esters. These are stronger than polyesters, cost about twice as much, have about the same viscosity, and cure about the same. Vinyl esters bond better than polyesters to Kevlar and carbon fiber. Vinyl esters have from 35 to 50 percent styrene content, and they require some different combinations of additives, which can actually cause an explosion if the mix sequence is improper! Derakane is one of the best known vinyl esters, available from Dow Chemical. Incidentally, there are many, many producers of resins. Your best bet to get quality is to talk to a local supplier and / or user. You can also con-tact the resin manufacturer for full information on product use and safety.

FIBERGLASS

Of itself, resin can be strong. By adding various kinds of fiber reinforcement, the resulting composite can have a degree of strength that can be useful for everything from kitchen tools to space craft. Fiber rein-forcements can be anything from carbon fiber to Nextel to 'glass to Kevlar to quartz or boron. Most any fiber could be a reinforcement, these are the most common.

Glass fibers are made by using heat and pressure, on a variety of materials, such as clay, limestone, gravel or sand. By varying the amounts of material in a mix, different kinds of glass (and resultant fiber) is created. Long filaments of glass fiber are created by drawing this melted glass through holes in the bottom of an electric furnace, (usually lots of holes for mass production). A single pound of glass can make a huge amount of filaments. Filament thickness will vary and different size filaments are mixed to create a strand.

Filaments are extremely tiny, there may be a couple thousand filaments in just one strand. A group of filaments can be twisted (same as with ordinary thread or rope) to form a strand, then strands can be twisted together. This yarn is then woven into a fiberglass cloth.

If the filaments are simply laid side by side (not twisted), the result is a roving fiber. This fiber is not as strong as a twisted fiber, but it can be woven the same way. This basket weave easily comes undone, it ranks between cloth and matte for a strength value, and it is commonly used in a laminate with matte for quick build-up in thickness.

The glass filaments are fragile, so during the weaving process an oil / starch binder may be included. This loom-state fiberglass must then be heated to burn off the binder. A common finish for car body fiberglass is a coating of methacrylic chromic chloride complex. The chrome finish makes fiberglass look shiny, a dull finish usually indicates a fabric you don't need. This chrome finish helps the resin to wet-out the fiberglass better, for an improved bond. Without a good finish, a structure of fiberglass and resin can lose most of its strength in a very short time. The bottom line is to use fiberglass that has a finish compatible with making car bodies, again you must rely on the supplier for help in selection. Most manufacturers of fiberglass have technical data that shows

exactly what each weave is for and the finish involved, they sometimes even recommend the kind of resin to use. The type of weave for cloth or roving can be a factor when strength is involved, and while this might be important on a race car chassis, it is not as vital in a car body. The most common types of weave are plain, satin, and unidirectional. Plain weave is what you normally find in the hardware store, a long shaft satin weave gives a very smooth finish and works well as the surface layer on car bodies and parts, while a unidirectional weave can be very effective in adding strength. It is possible to mix weaves in a single project.

The common types of fiberglass fabric used in a car body are cloth, roving, matte, and chopped strand. Cloth, roving, and matte fabrics are applied as a hand lay-up, chopped strand is applied with a special chopper gun, a production spray tool used by many commercial builders. The strength of the resin / fiberglass composite is affected by the 'glass as well as the resin. Since fiberglass cloth is woven the same as any woven fabric, strength depends on the style of the weave and thickness of the cloth. A good rule of thumb for car bodies and parts is a cloth from .010 to .015 inches thick, with a medium open weave (for resin penetration). Cloth also varies in weight per square yard, from under five pounds to

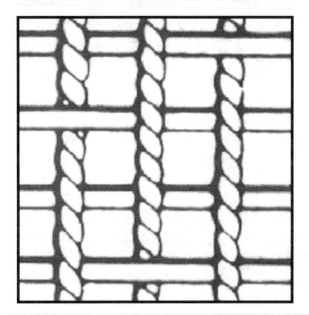

The three types of fabric weave most common to car building: Plain weave is the most simple, with each strand alternating over and under crossing strands. In a balanced weave the same number of strands go each way, in a unidirectional weave, more strands go one way than the other, greater strength is achieved in the direction of the most strands. The basket weave incorporates double strands to gain additional strength. The twill or satin weave has one yarn crossing over several yarns before going under a single yarn. Crossing over two yarns is called a twill, over three or four makes a crowfoot, over more than four it is a satin weave, etc. This type of weave gives a smooth surface finish.

more than 20 pounds per yard. For repair work, something in the range of six to 10 pounds is good, for construction of bodies and parts the weight can be heavier.

Woven roving does not saturate with resin as easily as either cloth or matte, but it requires less resin overall than matte, and it gives a much coarser surface than cloth. Roving is good for build-up, and it conforms to curves very well. It is harder to work with than cloth.

Matte is a mat. It consists of short lengths of filament in a haphazard ply, appearing as though a bunch of filaments had fallen on the floor. A refinement in matte has been to lay all the fibers in one direction, which increases end use strength considerably. By orienting one layer of matte 90 degrees to another layer and adding resin, even more strength is gained. Matte is not as strong as cloth, nor as expensive. It makes a good bulk-up filler, so many car parts are made of a layer of cloth, a layer of matte, and a final layer of cloth. A special surfacing matte is available that gives a much smoother finish than ordinary matte.

A chopper gun is a very quick way to add reinforced resin. Coiled strands of fiberglass are fed to a hand-held gun, which chops the strands into small pieces. A resin and catalyst mix is sprayed into the stream of fiberglass. An acetone supply keeps the gun nozzle clean. Essentially, this is an expensive production convenience. A fiberglass structure made with a chopper gun is not as strong as a hand lay-up part; some manufacturers follow a chopper gun application with some degree of hand lay-up, possibly even adding a layer of cloth.

EXOTIC FIBERS

There are plenty of other fibers in the general fiberglass field, but for the car enthusiast the least understood are what might be called the exotics. Carbon fiber fits this bill nicely, since it is widely used and little understood by the average car builder.

Carbon fibers (sometimes called graphite fibers) are made from strands of rayon or pan (polyacrylanitrile) that are oxidized, carbonized, and grafitized in a continuous, very closely controlled oven operation. They may also be made from pitch fibers, which come from petroleum or coal. As with most of the exotic fibers, you must work closely within a manufacturer's line to get consistency in your project. Polyester resins do not work well with carbon fibers, which really cuts down their selection on a typical car.

DuPont's Kevlar has very high strength with the added plus of being very tough. Weighing in at about half what aluminum weighs, Kevlar is used for bullet-proof vests, military armor, etc. Polyester resins do not work with Kevlar, either. Kevlar does not sand smooth, instead the resin sands away and the fiber strands stay behind. The more you sand the worse the case of hair. A thin layer of finishing cloth is the solution.

A really interesting new material has been created by 3M, called Nextel. It is slightly below 'glass in strength, but it has an extremely high resistance to heat (something in the range of 2,000 degrees F) and low heat transmission. Aircraft people think this is great for firewalls, it would probably work well for car firewalls and floors.

Polypropylene is a nonallergenic fabric that is lightweight with a high tensile strength. It is elastic, so that it works around curves very well, but it tends to float up in resin. Some extra work is necessary with this fabric. It has better abrasion resistance than 'glass, and it resists sanding. As with Dynel acrylic, Vectra polypropylene adheres to wood better than fiberglass (it is better than Dynel in this respect).

Dynel is from an acrylic yarn and weighs roughly half as much as fiberglass. Is is like polypropylene in many ways, giving a slick sanded finish, but it works in curved areas better than polypropylene. Because of the slick finish it works very well as a surface layer.

Like Dynel, Xynole polyester works around curves very well, but it lacks stiffness. It works as an overlay or as a waterproof coating.

MOCK-UPS, MOLDS, BUCKS, PLUGS, ETC.

MAKING THE THINGS FROM WHICH YOU MAKE THINGS

THE DESIGN

This is the point at which making car bodies and parts of fiberglass starts to get interesting. It

Get help designing from someone with that kind of talent. Many years ago, the author called on Art Center student and friend Steve Swaja to help design the HOT ROD MAGAZINE XR-6 project. Working from a known wheelbase and engine / transmission / rear end combination, Swaja created these ideas. Instructions were to include a fiberglass 1927 Ford Model T body cockpit, and go from there.

is also the point at which wannabe builders are separated from follow-through builders. You start spending a lot of time and money, so you might as well stop at this point unless you are really serious. You've got a work place, you've got the tools, and you know where to get the resin and fiberglass products quickly. Time to decide exactly what you are going to build.

You must already have decided on a chassis, at least the dimensions. You need to know, exactly, the tread width, the wheelbase, the general suspension travel, tire / wheel sizes, and ride height of the frame. It is also necessary to know the locations of the radiator, engine, transmission, and gas tank, give or take a couple of inches.

Whether you are going to make an entire car body, or just a part, you are going to be working with a mock-up (which will probably include a buck and may actually be a plug) and possibly a female mold. You are going to spend a lot of time at this point, and a fair amount of money on supplies. You are also faced with the dilemma of which type of vehicle and style to build, a decision that is actually the true starting point.

Not many car enthusiasts are going

Swaja, center, created a number of different styling treatments for the XR-6, including this one in clay being shown to initial body builder George Barris (left) and author Tex Smith (right).

to create an entirely new body style. Not many are going to build a complete body. A few are going to make up some pieces. Most are working with fiberglass bodies and parts they will purchase, or have already purchased, and they want to know the full story on how what they own has been made. And they want to know how to properly use what they have bought.

Very few car enthusiasts are good designers. In fact, very few customizers, amateur or professional, are good designers. Most are fair to excellent craftsmen, and many have a good eye for shapes. Anyone who wants to create a unique one-off body can benefit from help by an artist designer. A major amount of the really outstanding concept car business that flourishes in hot rodding and sports type kit cars is possible because there are a dozen or more really

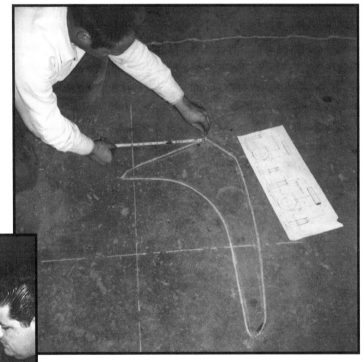

Working from design drawings supplied by Swaja, the outline of a pontoon fender is sketched on the shop floor. Although the final car was built in metal, it started out as a fiberglass assembly and outlines such as this worked fine for templates and parting flanges.

Working from photos of the completed car, plus on-site measurements, Budd Anderson and crew at AMT downsized the XR-6 into a plastic model kit. Reversing the procedure and making a full-sized car body from the plastic model is practical.

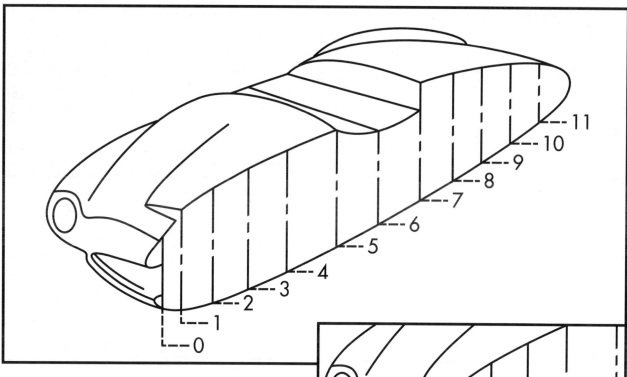

When designing a body, start with a model that is exact in every way, and perhaps as large as one-quarter scale. If you are creating something from clay, make the model one-half scale, if that is easiest. Cut the model apart at measured stations, side to side, to get template patterns, then enlarge these patterns to full size. Cut plywood templates from the patterns.

good designers at work on freelance projects. But, and this is the important point, too often overlooked, a designer does not necessarily have to work on your particular project. In fact, the designer doesn't even have to be alive.

It works like this. If there is a vehicle or a part that you want to reproduce, something that is not covered by some kind of copyright, that body or part is most likely the result of a designer, and can become your mock-up / plug / male mold. All those replicas of past designs that we generally lump under the heading of kit cars did not come from a fresh design and mock-up / buck / mold. Chances are a female mold was made from an original body or part. In the process, small changes in the original shape could easily be made. The

same scenario holds for most of the hot rod bodies available. Usually, a manufacturer of a hot rod body finds a very good original steel body. The original designer of that car may long since be gone, but the design is still good. Modifications can be made to the original body with materials that can be easily removed after a mold is made. In the case of a "phantom" project, a steel body in poor condition might be the foundation, with lots of changes made to suit the desired design. A phantom style is a body design that was never produced by a manufacturer originally. A sedan can become a phaeton, or a pickup roadster, or a classic style like no classic ever built. This is probably the most common kind of design, and definitely a salute to a good original style.

Often the templates can be attached directly to the intended chassis, but in this case students from the Art Center made a thick plywood floor plate and attached wheels to that. Then the templates were secured and this gives a good idea of what the body lines will be.

We'll get deeper into using these available shapes later, right now consider the problems of making something from scratch.

Let's assume that you have a great design you want to create in fiberglass. It is probably more along the lines of a sports car or a classic, and you can't find a body that you can highly modify to suit the purpose. This is a very important point, because you can sometimes find a body that has most of the lines you want, and all you must do is make modifications. Lots easier than creating a body from scratch. Get the word out that you are looking for a fiberglass body (let 'em know the general kind you want) and have a little patience. If all the fiberglass bodies ever produced commercially were turned into usable cars, the streets would be crowded with wonderful ideas.

So, no luck there and you have to make your own. If your design comes from an accomplished designer, you'll probably have dozens of different views to work from, and possibly even loftings. A lofting is the cross section shape of the body at various points from front to rear. If it is something that you've dreamed up in your head, with a couple of rough sketches on old Valvoline cartons, you need to do some additional brainstorming.

The most common method of making an idea into a visual piece is to cut apart pictures of cars that sort of look like what you have in mind. The hood and front fender area from one car, rear fenders from another, all this sectioned from front to back to get a leaner and lower

In this case, a frame of round tubing has been made and the wheels mocked into place, then plywood template formers created to give the final body shape. This is a buck, from which metal body panels can be made, or it can be turned into a mold mock-up.

line, and the top probably cut off. Not bad, especially for a non-designer. But this is the computer age, and you've got access to some Detroit-style help.

Someone in your community probably has access to a three-dimensional computer design program. Working from your crude sketch, or even outlines from your cut-apart photos, a skilled computer buddy can create exactly the shape you are looking for. Lines can be moved

at will, shapes changed and returned to original, instantly. Some of these CAD programs will even give you those loftings, or cross section outlines, which you can enlarge directly when making up a buck. A note at this point: Until you become something of an expert in producing fiberglass items, avoid lots of tight curves and tricky shapes. They will probably be very difficult to work with in the mold stage.

Four areas of a special body design will

Here the wooden buck is replaced by closed cell foam blocks that have been glued together then carved and sanded into a mock-up.

The lower half bellypan for this race car has been made, the upper body half can be laid up over the foam mock-up.

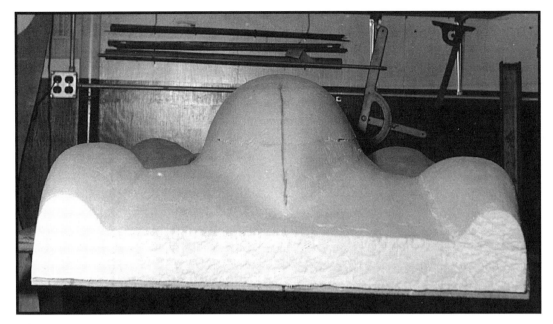

Foam is light and easy to carve, clay or plastic filler can be added to change shapes, just be sure and use foam that resins will not melt.

give you production problems, and the solutions are simply to design around something that is already available. First, you have need of a windshield, and chances are very good that you have something in mind that is shorter than those on most stock passenger cars. The windshield frame is something you can build, you must work around the glass. Scour junkyards and make templates, out there somewhere is a piece of glass that will work perfectly. It must be safety windshield glass, nothing else will do. Second, you'll probably use some part of a production grille, find what you need and work it into your mock-up. Same with a dashboard and the seats. Definitely pay attention to the seating area, building for drivers who range from 5 foot 5 inches to 6 foot 5 inches. The junkyard will yield an excellent assortment of adjustable seats, or you can get custom models from the street rod aftermarket. Same with an adjustable steering column, with a tilt / telescoping version a super choice to start with. Very clean versions of these columns are now available in street rodding circles. These are the parameters around which you will make your design work. Yes, there are some really high-dollar concept cars hitting the show circuit every year that have all these features custom made. Most of them have builder fees in the neighborhood of a quarter million

dollars. Or more. Your choice.

If you are not totally confident in going from a good computer design, or even those Valvoline carton scribbles, directly to a full-size mock-up, you can make up a scale model first. Some really nice fiberglass designs have been achieved by working with modelling clay over a plastic model. The model can be sectioned and chopped and given all kinds of preliminary work, then the clay smooths all the rough edges. In essence, the model becomes a miniature buck. Just remember that the larger the model you work with, the easier it is for you to pick out problem areas that might not form so easily from the mold. In a very real way, this type of clay modelling is one of the steps taken by professional automobile designers, except that they usually end up making a full-sized clay model. If you get really hung up on this design phase of making a fiberglass car, you'll want to study our book *How To Draw Cars.*

You can use a model to advantage if you need to make up lofting stations. If you finish off the clay (or whatever) on the model, you can then make a plaster cast of one side of the model. You only mold one side, since your clay model is now a plug and you need the cast to pull off the plug. Suggestion, add plaster to water, not water to plaster, and mix so that you do not have lumps. When the plaster hardens, you have a female mold. From this you can use more plaster and make up a male mold. Working with either the female or male mold, you can get the shapes of each lofting station. Most cars will have a wheelbase from around 95 to 125 inches, the actual body may be longer (in the case of a sports car or classic) or shorter (in the case of a very few hot rods). Each lofting station on a buck or mold mock-up will usually be from 8 to 12 inches apart.

Determine the size ratio of the model to the real car, and you know where each lofting station cross section will be. Cut the plaster cast (either female or male) apart at each of these stations, and you have a cross section outline of one side of the design. Trace this on paper, flop the tracing, and you have a complete cross section. Enlarge this to whatever ratio you are working with, and you have a full-sized former plan that can be transferred to plywood or whatever medium you are working with. If all the stations are lined up the correct distance apart, you have the basis of a buck (for making a metal body) or a full-sized mock-up.

THE MOCK-UP / PLUG / BUCK

So, some definitions. A mock-up is something you make that looks like what you want. It can be a table-top model, or it can be life-size. A plug is something that is life size, from which you make either the fiberglass part you want, or a female mold. In a way, it is the same as the mock-up, if you work directly from the mock-up to make a part or a mold. A buck is not normally considered the same as a fiberglass mock-up, although a mock-up might go through the buck stage as it becomes a mock-up. A buck is usually something made of wood or wire that gives the general outlines of a body or piece, and over which metal pieces are shaped. Let's see, a better description. When a stick and tissue model airplane is built, the uncovered balsa wood stringers and formers would be a buck. From this stage, the buck can become a mock-up if tissue or clay or something else is added to the stringers and formers, then this overlay is shaped to a design from which a fiberglass part can be made. It's the same as the plastic model with a clay overlay mentioned previously.

The problem with working from a model of

PRESSURE MOLDS

When it is desirable to create a lot of fiberglass units with a smooth finish on both sides, such as with the Corvette, pressure molds are used. These assemblies look much like a metal stamping die set, in that there is a smooth interior female mold and a smooth exterior male mold. The fiberglass and resin (or in some cases a more exotic mixture), are placed into the female mold, then the male mold is inserted. A relatively light pressure is applied, to ensure a uniform thickness of resin / glass, and usually the mold is subjected to heat to accelerate and ensure maximum cure. Obviously, this is a very costly process, even for the production of a few hundred units.

Another form of pressure molding is called vacuum bagging, wherein the entire contents of a laid-up mold are enclosed in a bag, then all the air is evacuated from the bag. This allows atmospheric pressure (around 14 psi) to become the external pressure. This method is not as expensive as the two-mold approach, but enough of a bother that most builders leave it to aircraft fiberglass projects.

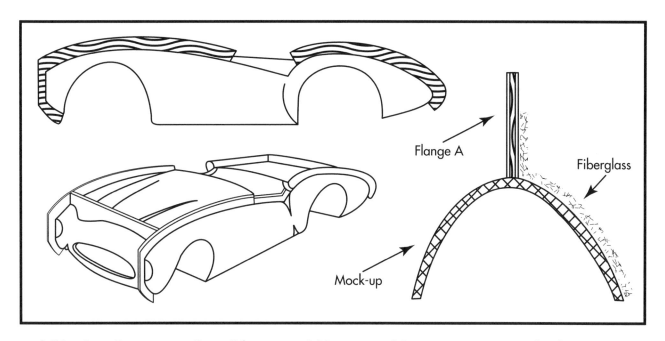

Flange A

Fiberglass

Mock-up

A full body will not normally pull from a mold because of the many curves involved. Parting flanges made of plywood or metal must be made to fit the mock-up precisely. As each section of female mold is fiberglassed in place, the matching parting flanges are included. Each flange (A) consists of two separate but matching pieces held together by bolts and nuts.

the body design is that the chassis / engine / interior may not have been considered. Building a chassis to fit a body is not nearly as easy as fitting a body to an existing chassis. When you are making up a mold using an existing body (an old Model T coupe body, for instance) you know what chassis and engine combinations will work. Not so with a body style unlike any previous design. For this reason alone, it is wise to get a rolling chassis ready. The preliminary drawings may show that the engine can be relocated (usually to the rear) several inches, and the cockpit may be set just ahead of the rear wheels. The suspension can be modified to lower the entire vehicle several inches. Most all this information can be figured out and a chassis roughed into

Parting flanges are placed so that the mold can be taken apart and removed from the initial mock-up, and from subsequent fiberglass bodies.

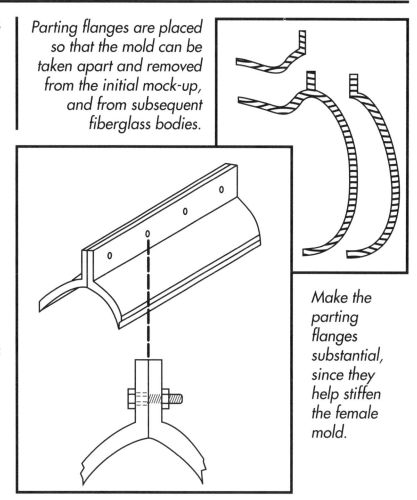

Make the parting flanges substantial, since they help stiffen the female mold.

shape. The body is then designed to clear all these chassis pieces, including radiator, engine, seats, and gas tank.

If a body is created without a chassis, the station loft templates are attached along some kind of backbone, this backbone is often on casters. If a chassis is involved, each template can have the inner area cut away for clearance, but the template must be securely attached to the frame temporarily. In general, this is the way most custom builders create one-off designs.

It should be noted here that for one-off designs, it is not uncommon for a builder to start with a rolling chassis and build minimal size rectangular station formers along the

length. These formers become mounting points for templates that are shaped, and reshaped, until the builder reaches a desirable design mock-up. This cut and try method works okay if the builder has a really good ability to imagine what is to be built, or an artist is available for periodic consultation.

Since each side of the body should be identical in shape, make a centerline on the mock-up. This centerline can be marked by placing nails in the midpoint of each station template, each nail sticking up well above the mock-up finish, from which a carpenter's chalk line can be stretched. Each nail will be removed before the mock-up gets a finish prior

This is the full passenger side female mold for a 1929 Ford roadster from Gibbon Fiberglass. Note that the door opening, with jambs, is included in the mold, the doors are molded separately. For production purposes, the mold has stiffening ribs on the quarter panel area.

This Model A Ford rear fender female mold at Poli-Form has been created with a finish gel coat on the inside so that the fiberglass fender will have a perfectly smooth surface. The outside of the mold is not vital, thus strands of matte are ignored, the entire mold mounts on a solid wood support frame.

to making a body or a mold.

The templates are really just guide stations, therefore something is needed to give a foundation for the mock-up "skin," which can be made from plaster of paris, similar material available from a pattern-making shop, or foam. With plaster, a chicken wire base can be formed over the templates, but this woven wire really needs a base for strength. Ordinary bailing wire can be run back and forth between the templates, or wood stringers can be installed between templates. Anything to make a foundation for the chicken wire. Once the chicken wire is stapled in place, it can be pushed and pulled to give the general outlines of the body or part.

When using plaster, mix the plaster into the water and stir constantly to get a smooth mix. The

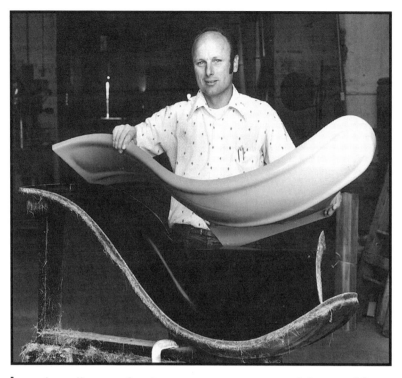

Dick Williams of Poli-Form removes a Model T Ford front fender from the mold. The finished part is primed and painted as would be a metal part, the mold is good for a long production run before being replaced.

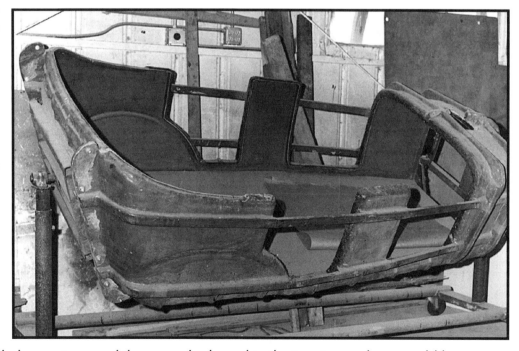

This is a mold for a 1927 Model T Ford touring body. Note the wood and metal reinforcement bands around the outside of the body to eliminate distortion, giving the entire mold enough strength to allow mounting on a rotating base. In years past, the T bodies were molded one-piece and then wood 'glassed to the interior so doors could be cut out with a sabre saw. Now openings are put in the body and the doors are made separately. It's more work, but a much better body is the result. Note that here the parting flanges are at the center of the cowl and at both sides of the rear panel. This gives enough draft for easy mold release from the body, and allows the door jambs to be molded in place.

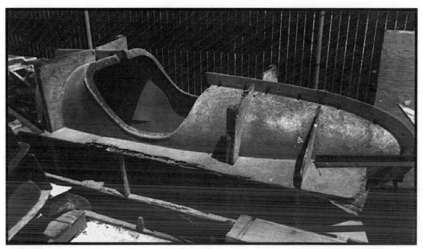

Note the parting flanges and supporting spars on this Poli-Form female mold. Such well-built molds can be stored for years.

plates, bridging the gaps. This will scrape away the high spots, and give a very good conformation of the plaster to the template guides. On all but the final layer of plaster, use something to give directional ridges. These ridges help subsequent plaster bite better, and when running the spline over the surface you get a better idea of high and low spots. A plastic tool used for floor tile adhesives works, as does a carpenter's cross-cut saw blade. After the plaster sets, add still another layer, which will be thin or non-existent in some spots and thick in low areas. Bring the plaster up until it is just below the template edges, the final layer of plaster should be level with each template. Use the flexible tool (the straight backside of that carpenter's saw is good) to scrape the moist plaster into a semi-finished shape. After the plaster has set, use a "cheese grater" on one side of the mock-up to get the exact final shape you want. This is the kind of grater used to work plastic body filler, work with the longest one you can find for this initial shaping.

Make female templates from cardboard to fit the finished side, then shape the off side to these templates. This should insure that you have a body that is the same on both sides. Lots of work, yes, but you've only started.

plaster hardness depends on your ratio of plaster powder to water, you'll want the final layer to be hard enough to resist dings but soft enough for easy sanding. Do some experiments on powder / water ratios and then stick with the same ratio throughout. Dip pieces of cheesecloth in the plaster, drape this saturated cloth on the chicken wire, and pull it taut. Smooth it enough so that there are no great jagged edges sticking above the template body line. Do the entire body or part, and let it dry for six to eight hours.

The idea is to use just enough plaster or Calcerite to accept shaping, with each station template as a guide for thickness. The second layer of plaster does not include the cheese-cloth. While it is still wet, run something over the surface to shape the plaster. If you work a couple of template gaps at a time, you can run a long flexible piece of metal or wood across three of the tem-

This is a 1934 Ford three-window coupe body curing after hand lay-up. The female mold pieces are bolted together so the body can not warp during the extended curing phase.

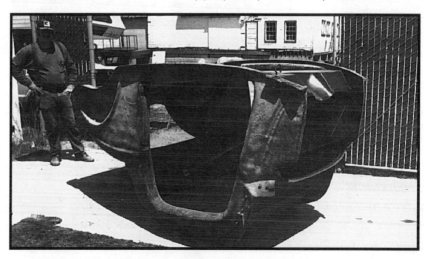

An alternate to a plaster mock-up is the use of rigid closed-cell foam blocks or sheets, the kind of foam used in building insulation, for floating docks, etc. There are three types used with fiberglass: polyvinyl chloride (PVC), polystyrene and polyurethane. Only polyvinyl chloride and polyurethane work with polyester resins. Do not use styrofoam.

Foam can be shaped with a saw, sanded, and is easy to form. If a mistake is made, a piece of surplus foam is glued in place and the area is shaped again. This foam can be left in place, but the result is a rough exterior that requires a tremendous amount of sanding and filling. Of course, the foam (in block, sheet, or foam-in-place types) is an excellent agent if a sandwich laminate is needed wherein sheer strength is not paramount. Overall, foam is best suited for making a mock-up.

In the freehand type of mock-up, the foam is attached to the bare chassis (or a flat piece of plywood on a flat floor / table), pieces glued together to get enough mass for carving. Or, the foam blocks may be glued between the mock-up templates. The foam is then carved

Once the Poli-Form body is cured, the mold is separated at all the parting flanges. A good release agent and firm but gentle pressure ensures that the mold comes off.

with an electric carving knife (the kind used for Thanksgiving turkey works dandy) or with a hot electric wire element (the kind model airplane builders use). A thin coat of plaster or plastic filler makes the foam smooth and gives a surface for final shaping, probably using layers of plastic filler or resin. The foam selected must be a composition that will not be melted by polyester resin.

Seal the plaster surface with something like shellac or with a thin layer of resin. Sand the sealed surface smooth. Then it is time to lay on a coat of lacquer primer. Put this primer coat on thick, then sand with 220 sandpaper, using long sanding blocks to get the truest possible finish. Add more filler as needed until the surface is perfect, then more primer and more block sanding. Finally, paint the surface with a good acrylic lacquer. Any dark color

The passenger side of the mold has been removed. The mold pieces are very rigid and quite heavy.

Here the windshield and header mold is gone. Note that a thin film of fiberglass was laid up in the windshield opening. This will be trimmed out, as will all the edges.

will show imperfections that were not caught before. When these are fixed, and more paint applied, the mock-up is finished. Bear in mind that the finished body or part will only be as good as the mock-up and the mold.

This mock-up could actually be a final mold, with fiberglass laid over the surface. But the result would be a body extremely rough on the outside and mirror smooth on the inside. Instead, use the mock-up as a plug, from which to make a female mold.

Cost is a factor. If only one body or part is to be made, it may be tempting to mold over the mock-up plug and try to smooth the rough fiberglass surface. In the long run, however, the extra effort will more than offset the extra cost of making a female mold. Materials needed to make a female mold are approximately equal to that needed to make the final body, and the total cost of the mock-up and molds will be several times what the body material will be. There is also the possibility the female mold might be used by a buddy, or even sold to a manufacturer. As a rule, a well-built female mold is good for up to 100 bodies.

The strength of the female mold is vital. If it is necessary to make the mold in two or more sections (in order to remove the final molded part), you must make parting flanges (usually of wood). Flanges should also be added around any open edges for reinforcement. Parting

flanges should be several inches in height, and conform to the mock-up's contours exactly. At each parting line, there will be two flanges. These are bolted together and subsequent layers of fiberglass cover the mock-up and run up the sides of the flanges. After the female mold is cured, the sections unbolt. When the final body is made, the mold can again be disassembled for ease in release. A major advantage of making up a mold in sections is that door jambs and hood / deck lid recesses can be molded as the body is made. Of course, this means that individual molds must then be made for hood, deck lid, and doors. In the past, it has been common to mold an entire body, then cut the hood, deck, and doors from the body, using a sabre saw. This procedure is covered in detail later. The problem is that unless the section being cut away, as well as adjoining body areas, is supported by an inner substructure, distortion of the cut-out part can occur. Getting a really good fit is the result, so it is usually better to make separate molds for movable body parts.

There are two kinds of molding: contact and pressure. Pressure is the type where a plug is pressed against a mold, similar to forming sheet metal on a press. Both the plug and the mold have a smooth surface, so the part is smooth on both sides without lots of sanding. This is the kind of molding used by manufacturers that need a high-production run.

Contact molding is what the average builder uses, with the weight of the resin and fiberglass cloth against the mold surface supplemented by hand pressure. In this method, hand lay-up and spray (chopper gun) lay-up are used.

The mock-up surface must be as smooth as the final body surface is to be. The painted and polished surface should be waxed with a top quality carnuba, polished, and waxed again. Over this wax, apply a parting agent, which you may buy from any good fiberglass materials supplier. If you make your own:

- Polyvinyl alcohol
  Dissolve in hot water,
  Apply by brush or spray

- Cellulose acetate molding compound
  Mix ½ pound cellulose acetate compound to 1 gallon acetone
  Brush or spray

- Carboxy methyl cellulose
  Dissolve 1-2 percent carboxy methyl cellulose in 1 gallon hot water
  Brush or spray

Apply two coats of parting agent, with an hour's drying time between coats. After the second coat of parting agent has dried, apply more carnuba wax and polish. You are now ready to create a female mold.

On production fiberglass, the shiny surface is the result of a gel coat, which is simply pure resin that may or may not have a color included. This same gel coat is used in the female mold to get a perfectly smooth surface. Since the gel coat is mixed to set in about 30 minutes, mix up a pint at a time. This pint will go a long way. Spray or brush (spray is best) this resin on the entire mock-up, don't miss anywhere. It will be runny, so expect a mess. A couple of coats won't hurt.

The body side mold includes door jambs and roll for the floor. Metal floors can be installed, but most builders opt for a fiberglass or plywood floor.

Back to the work area for a moment. Space is a pleasure, when working with fiberglass. Assuming that you have the mock-up with plenty of work room, create a big workbench nearby. Something about 8 feet long by 4 feet wide is nice. Cover the bench with cellophane or anything that the resin won't ruin. You are going to saturate your various fiberglass layers on this bench and then move each laminate to the mock-up, a procedure you will duplicate when making the actual body. It takes about a quart of resin to impregnate 2 square feet of cloth.

You will be doing the large body in segments, not all at once (unless you have several helpers) and work each section until the resin has gelled. The first layer will be cloth. Pick an area at the top of the mock-up (deck lid, hood, etc). Lay out a piece of cloth about 3 x 3 feet on the workbench, and saturate this with catalyzed resin, working the resin evenly into the cloth with a squeegee or blade. Protect your hands with rubber gloves, and have plenty of acetone handy for clean-up. Methyl ethyl keytone is a better cleaning compound. Lay the saturated section of fiberglass on the top of the mock-up and work out the air bubbles. The adjoining layer of cloth should overlap the first by an inch or so, and at the edges of all openings there should be an extension of an

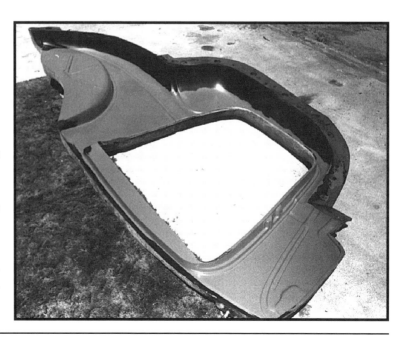

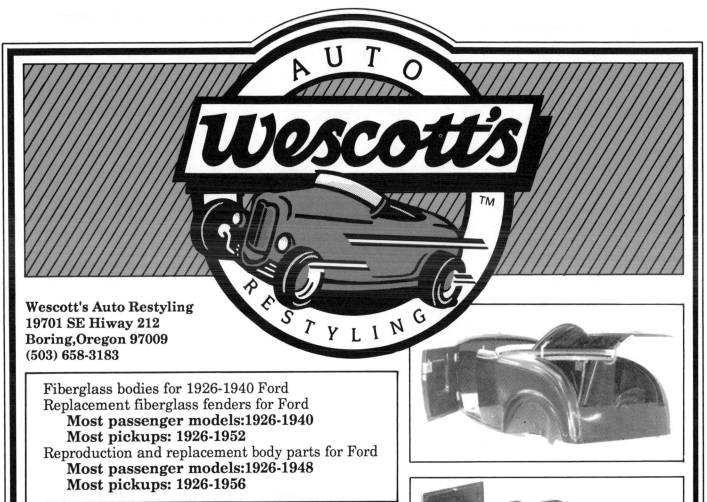

inch or two for later trim. Work out trapped air with the squeegee, you do not want any voids or air bubbles in this initial layer of fiberglass reinforcement. Very important. As you work, the resin will run to the low spots, move it back with a brush, this redistribution will continue until the resin kicks.

The next layer will be matte, more than one layer in large flatter sections. You can add several layers of matte if you want. The final layer is fiberglass cloth. You can lay the cloth on the workbench, then the matte, and saturate both before applying to the mock-up. Or you can lay dry matte on the cured first layer of cloth, then the final layer of dry cloth, and saturate this combination in place on the mock-up. It will take a gallon of polyester resin to saturate a square yard of matte / cloth. Work out all the air bubbles that you can. Do not remove the mold for several days, to avoid distortion during curing. For ease of working with the female mold, attach some sort of support to the mold (square metal tubing, wood, etc) and add some casters. Attach the support structure at body curves or at parting flanges, never at large flat areas. When the female mold is removed from the mock-up, and turned upside down you then have a solid support.

If you want to take the time, make a rotisserie for the mold. This is a framework that allows the mold to revolve around the mold centerline. Thus, as the body is being laid up in the mold, it can be swung so that the area being worked is always flat. Production body builders use these kinds of revolving supports.

Even when a large body female mold is made with parting flanges, getting the fiberglass sections to release from the mock-up may require smooth wooden wedges lightly tapped between mock-up and mold, or tap the mold with a rubber mallet. Clean the mold thoroughly with acetone, then look for any air pockets. Stick a pin in each air pocket, collapse it, and finish with resin and filler. Make the repair perfectly smooth. Sand the mold surface with 180 wet / dry sandpaper and you are ready to make a body.

A special note: If the body is to be fitted with separate doors, deck lid, hood, etc, it is necessary to make separate molds for each piece. It is also necessary to form the openings on the mock-up and in the female mold. This takes planning, but it results in a very professional finished product.

The final product, which Poli-Form workers inspect carefully. Minor imperfections are easily repaired if necessary, but block sanding is necessary to get a typical body up to show quality in preparation for paint.

MAKING PATTERNS AND TEMPLATES

While it is very convenient to have full-scale drawings and loftings of a proposed car body or part, that procedure is often way out of the economic league of the amateur fiberglass builder. In this chapter we mention use of a model as the early-on phase of both design and mock-up creation. If you start the process with a hobby shop plastic model, the model normally is marked as to what ratio it is to full size, such as one-tenth scale, or one-twenty fifth, etc. Thus you know your starting point when making patterns and templates for a full-sized body or part. If you are going to change the model body lines with clay or plastic filler, the larger the model size you start with the more accurate will be these changes as you make patterns.

Wayne Yeats has been involved with all forms of specialty cars for years, but he is best known for fiberglass pedal car bodies. Although these bodies are much smaller than a full-sized counterpart, their creation follows the same steps outlined in this book, he just stops short of making a full-sized unit. The procedure that Yeats uses will apply to anything made of fiberglass, if the starting point is a model.

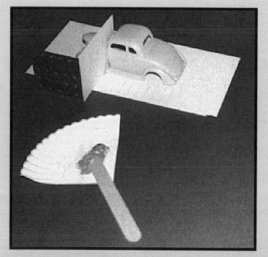

A one-twenty-fifth-scale 1936 Ford coupe model is the starting point for a one-third-scale fiberglass roadster body for a pedal car chassis. The model, without wheels, is attached to a stiff base which has station lofting locations marked. The model is heavily coated with good carnuba car wax, and polished. Some .030-inch thick styrene sheet from a model shop is rough cut to fit each lofting station, from the side to the centerline of the body.

Ordinary body repair plastic filler is mixed in small quantities and is spread from the lofting station template to the body. This gives the exact shape of the body. After the filler has hardened, it is removed from the model and sanded smooth on both sides. This pattern is pasted to a sheet of black paper, then a corresponding female pattern is rough cut and positioned adjacent, so that only a small irregular black line shows between the two pieces of white styrene. This is done so that when using a photocopier to enlarge the pattern excess ink in the copier is not wasted. One pattern for a future template is ready, it is marked for location and set aside.

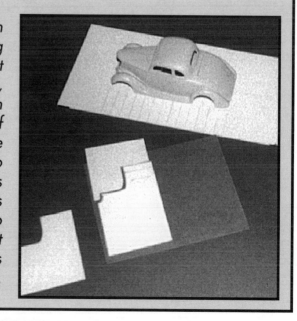

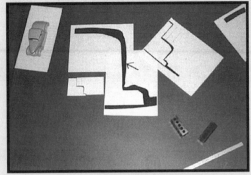

The exact contour of the model body is the outside line, that is where the cut is made. Since the model was made by scaling down a full-sized car, the reverse procedure should be very accurate.

In this procedure, a body contour has been taken from the small model, enlarged on a photocopier, from one-twenty fifth scale up to one-third scale.

The pattern can be traced on posterboard or plywood, and either a female or male template is the result.

Wayne Yeats shows the 1936 Ford grille as cast in fiberglass from a female mold created from patterns.

This is the "full size" one-third scale fiberglass pedal car body made from the one-twenty fifth-scale plastic model. The coupe top was eliminated during the mock-up stage and replaced by the open roadster styling, making a full-sized car with similar changes would be done the same way.

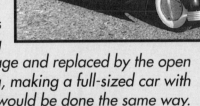

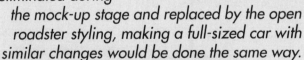

Fiberglass pedal car version of Norm Grabowski's famous Kookie II touring. The real car was made from a two-door Model A sedan, if a production fiberglass body were made it would have the female mold taken directly from the car, but it could be duplicated from a small plastic model as we have shown.

MAKING BODIES AND PARTS

USING THE THING YOU MADE TO MAKE THE THING YOU WANT

How you can make the thing you started out needing (or wanting), the body or some individual parts. While all the work of creating a mock-up and building a female mold may seem a lot of effort and expense, the result shows in the product. And what you get as a completed fiberglass body or part will be an exact mirror of the female mold.

Which is the reason that once the female mold has cured and been taken from the mock-up it is imperative that the mold surface be inspected inch by inch. Imperfections must be removed. Air pockets can be punctured, then repaired with plastic filler and sanded perfectly smooth. A glitch in the design can be modified at this time, with fiberglass and filler. It is all a matter of patience and working through a sanding routine that ends with 600 grit sandpaper. The mold surface can then be polished, before adding wax or release agent.

Polyester resin never stops shrinking. No matter how well the female mold is supported with external reinforcements, this shrinking continues. It is a tiny amount, but it is forever. This is another reason that manufacturers replace molds through the years.

A reminder that laying up fiberglass and resin works best on a level / nearly level surface. The resin does not stay readily in place on a vertical or overhead surface, no matter what the viscosity. This is why a female mold should be made that can be rotated about the body axis, with the working access usually through the floor / door / deck lid openings. In larger production runs, the female mold can be designed to attach to a rotisserie, and several workers lay up a horizontal section before rotating the mold. For limited production, the mold's parting flanges will

Once the mold is waxed and a parting agent has been applied (and dried), a gel coat of resin is brushed or sprayed over the entire mold. If there is any oil on the mold beneath the parting agent, the agent will not lay smooth against the mold. The area on the mold must be cleaned and new parting agent applied. Usually about one ounce of gel coat is required to cover one square foot. Do the entire mold with gel coat.

Apply resin to the gel-coated mold only in an area that can be worked easily; for one person that is normally from three to five square feet at a time. Until you get the procedure worked out, it is best to have less resin than fiberglass for this initial stage, since more resin can be added as needed. Over the resin lay the first layer of fiberglass weave cloth. Saturate this layer of fiberglass completely, working out all the air bubbles.

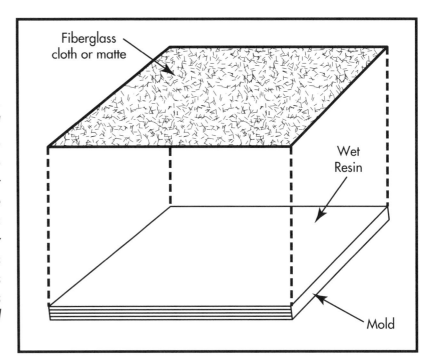

Fiberglass cloth or matte

Wet Resin

Mold

usually be strong enough to support the upturned mold.

Making the actual fiberglass body, or any kind of parts, follow nearly the same procedure in lay-up as in making the mold. Give the female mold from four to five really good wax coats, polishing each one to a sheen. This fills the microscopic holes in the mold, but you don't want any excess wax hanging around. Next, add a release agent, which you get from the materials supplier. While it is possible to carefully apply this agent with a brush, you will get the best results with a spray gun. This is a water soluble agent, and you want a very thin, uniform coating on every part of the female mold surface. Assuming that you have a female mold created from several bolted-together molds, be sure and spray the mating flange surfaces so everything comes apart at a later time. If the parting agent doesn't want to adhere to the mold, suspect grease contamination, which must be removed completely to get the release agent to work. Allow the parting agent to dry for an hour or so before continuing. Obviously, protect the mold from contamination or debris.

The fiberglass fabric to be used in the body or parts lay-up is a fairly straightforward selection. Cloth will be an open square weave, at about 8 ounces per

Use an up-down dabbing motion with a brush to get out the air bubbles and thoroughly saturate the fiberglass. This is especially effective with matte to avoid disruption of the random fiber layers.

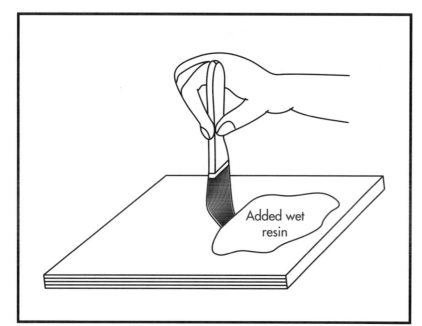
Added wet resin

The layers of fiberglass in a typical car body will be cloth / matte / roving. After each layer is applied, new resin is spread. Remember only a three to five square foot area is laid up at a time.

square foot. This weave can be pulled and compressed in tight curved areas without ruffling. Be absolutely certain that the cloth is not contaminated with grease or dirt, and that it has been "finished."

While it is possible to build up a laminate with successive layers of cloth, cloth alone gives a rather flexible laminate. Car bodies and parts are usually made of a sandwich, made of one layer of cloth, one or two layers of matte (or chopped fibers), and a final layer of cloth. Cloth gives strength, the matte provides bulk, 2 ounce per square foot matte is common. Cloth is available in bulk widths of 38, 50, 60, and 72-inches (sometimes wider) as well as one-half-to 6-inch-wide "tape," you'll probably want some of the narrow tape on hand for working the smaller areas. These narrow tapes have woven edges that resist fraying, which can be especially annoying when working with carbon fiber or Kevlar. By cutting the cloth and matte into working pieces and having them ready, lay-up is speeded (and a lot less messy).

It is imperative that the mixing of resin be accurate, particularly any epoxies. Follow the manufacturer instructions! By being consistent in mix ratios, only ambient temperatures and humidity become variables to setting time and quality of laminate strength.

Once the parting agent has dried thoroughly, the gel coat can be sprayed into the mold. This coating can be colored, but experienced builders agree that the results are not as good as a traditional painted finish. For spraying, mix the gel coat with three times the normal amount of catalyst (6 percent instead of 2 percent) and thin with styrene. This is not a regular resin coat, you get it at your 'glass materials supply house. Hold the spray gun about twice the normal distance from the surface, or about 16 inches. If the gel coat is applied with a brush, mix with the normal ratio. Either way, keep the gel coat thin. This gel coat is the shiny surface the body or part will exhibit before finishing, and it prevents the fiberglass from coming to the surface. At a later time, when sanding the body or part, be careful not to sand through the gel coat. If you do, add a spot layer of resin before proceeding to the painting stage.

It is now time to start the fiberglass lay-up. Most builders lay the fiberglass-resin composite directly into the female mold. In the event you elect to saturate the glass or matte on a table and transfer it to the mold, be advised not to use any kind of waxed paper. The wax will work through the resin and become a release. Instead, use a ply of plastic film as the table cover. Pick up the saturated cloth or matte with the plastic film and invert the layer in the mold. The plastic can then be an air shield during use of a squeegee. More on that shortly.

Two types of polyester resins are commonly used to make bodies and parts. The lay-up or laminating resin is air inhibited, which means it does not completely cure in the presence of air. The exposed surface remains tacky. This is the resin that will be used for all but the final coat of resin. Finishing or surfacing resin is non-air inhibited, so it will completely cure in the presence of air. This kind of resin has a wax (or similar ingredient) included that rises to the surface after application to seal off air and allow complete curing. If this sealing surface must be removed for additional lamination, acetone will do the job, as will sanding. While there are general purpose resins available, and they work okay on smaller parts, something as large as a body is best done with both types of resin. Incidentally, it is possible to cover the lay-up resin with something like cellophane (tape the edges to keep out air) to promote a complete cure, thus no tacky surface. As a matter of information, it is possible to add a co-reactant compound to the resin that will give fire retardation. Normal fiberglass structures burn readily, not so with this retardant.

Assuming you'll do direct lay-up in the mold, one person can usually work only about three to five square feet at a time. This means that you'll be overlapping each successive section as you go along. If the preceding section has not kicked when you add the next section, overlap about six inches at each "wet seam." If the preceding section has kicked, you'll need to sand the overlap area down to the cloth or matte fibers before adding the next section. This will insure a good bond.

You should always test the resin / catalyst mix ratio. The larger the amount being mixed, the greater will be the exothermic (heating) to the chemical reaction. A large amount of resin will kick sooner than half the amount, etc. If too much catalyst is added, the resin can actually generate enough heat to ignite! This is why you need to know exactly what the resin mixing ratio is. This ratio can then be modified slightly to account for working area temperature … the cooler the temperature the more catalyst can be added, the hotter the temperature, the less catalyst. Within limits, of course. This is why you make a test with polyester resin before attacking the actual lay-up. Remember that the mixing ratio of epoxy resin must always be exact, no deviation from directions.

Put a section of fiberglass weave cloth in place, and add the catalyzed resin. This is usually poured over the cloth, and the resin is thoroughly mashed into the cloth weave. A squeegee works well for this (as do some special rollers), mash and pull the squeegee to force the resin into the cloth, don't use too much force and flatten the "springy" resin / glass mixture. If you do, the cloth weave will spring up behind the squeegee. You do not want this exposed cloth surface. The ideal surface will be just enough resin to barely cover the cloth. Learning the approximate amount of resin needed to saturate a certain size section will take a couple of attempts, but

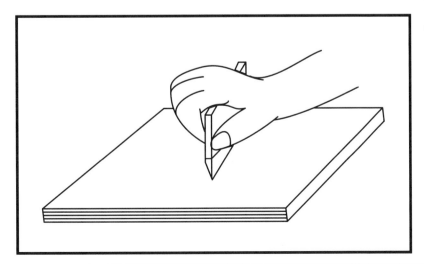

After the fiberglass is in place and thoroughly saturated with resin, excess resin and air bubbles are worked out with a squeegee. For this type of lay-up, the ratio should be 50 percent fiberglass to 50 percent resin. Excess resin should be removed, after some practice there will be very little excess.

When the next and succeeding sections of laminate are added to the mold, each laminate should overlap the preceding section by about six inches. Sand the preceding overlap if it has hardened, if it is tacky, no sanding is required.

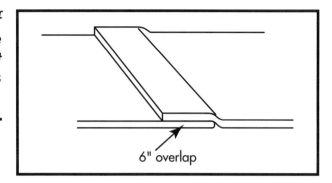

6" overlap

it is better to mix too little resin than waste excess. You can also saturate the cloth or matte by stippling the resin overlay with a stiff brush. This is an up / down motion with the brush same as with stencilling, the idea being to drive the resin down between the glass fibers. The alternative is to cover the section working area with resin, and lay the glass on top. The stippling action of a brush pushes the glass fibers into the resin. This method produces less air bubbles than does resin over glass.

Fill the 'glass fibers completely, if you don't the result will be a bluish-white appearance. Add more resin to that area and work it in. Remove excess resin from any mold area that is not covered with fiberglass. The strength is from the 'glass, not resin. Excess resin merely adds excess weight and cost. In a vacuum mold or mating mold pressure layup, the resin / glass ratio will be about 25 percent resin. In the open layup described here, the ratio will be just about 50 percent resin and 50 percent 'glass (by weight). Thus, you can weigh the 'glass and resin to get an idea of amount needed. These ratios will be different for the more exotic reinforcements, such as carbon fibers. A materials supplier will help you determine ratios if you get into different fibers.

Air bubbles are easy to get in polyester resins. Do not use a rapid stirring motion when mixing, and do not use a power mixer. You can see air bubbles trapped in the resin, the fewer bubbles you create during mixing, the better. These bubbles must be worked out of the resin as you spread it on the fiberglass, which you can do with the squeegee. But, you'll notice that the squeegee itself can also trap air, which is why some people like to lay cellophane or PVC plastic film over freshly applied resin. The squeegee can be pulled over this surface

without adding air. It takes a bit of practice to get the squeegee technique just right. You can also buy a special additive for the resin that reduces air bubble entrapment.

Working on a flat (horizontal) surface will seem reasonably easy with the typical resin, and you'll have enough time to work a section thoroughly before the resin starts to harden. Clean your tools (everything that has been subjected to catalyized resin) immediately, before starting the next section. Do not wash your hands in acetone. If resin hardens on any metal tools, it is nearly impossible to remove. On surfaces approaching vertical, the thin resin will tend to run out of the 'glass, so you must constantly mop the resin back over the 'glass until the resin starts to harden. This is tiring, and seldom really effective, which is why you should move the mold as you work to keep a nearly horizontal platform. You can buy a resin with a thicker viscosity, which is simply a mix using special thixotropic powder, or you can buy the powder and add to the resin you have. Do not use clay or inert dirt. Do some experiments before laying on too much. Patience, patience, patience.

At every edge (opening) let the fiberglass protrude past the edge an inch or so. Just after the resin starts to kick (for about ten minutes), you can trim the excess cloth or matte very easily with a sharp knife or razor blade. (The exotics don't trim as easily, for them you'll need special hardened tools.) If you wait too long and the resin has completely cured, you'll have to use a grinder, a cut-off wheel, hacksaw, or a jig saw. It's much, much easier to get the trimming done early on.

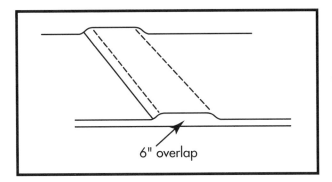

6" overlap

Work the overlap to reduce the edge, make sure all the fibers are covered with resin and flattened.

Once the entire mold has been covered with a layer of resined fiberglass cloth, let it set for awhile. The resin used at this stage stays tacky, you're just waiting for the first layer to thoroughly kick. For the typical body, a layer of multi-directional matte comes next. The thicker this matte, the stronger will be the body. On large areas where a little extra strength seems needed, add a second layer of matte—same around flanges or openings. While it is true that strength is related to the thickness of the 'glass, a normal car body needs only the mentioned three layers. If, at a later date, you determine that an area needs more strength, sand that area and add more 'glass.

It is usually easiest to brush on a coat of resin and lay the matte in place, then saturate the matte and work out the air bubbles. Follow the same procedure as with the first layer of cloth.

The final layer of cloth can be the open weave you used first, or a roving (18 ounce works well). Do this layer exactly as the first two layers. But, the last thing you will do is add a coat of resin that contains an additive to make it tack free (not sticky), and to be really trick, a black pigment to disguise the glass.

Curing time for a body or part may seem to be about 24 hours, but even production shops are at odds on this time. Some people say that when the composite cures, it is cured, period. Others like to let a body stay in the mold for much longer. The longer the better, several days at least. Most agree that if substructures are to be added, it is best to have the body in the mold to avoid distortion. This isn't always possible, however. We get into this in a

subsequent chapter.

If the body has been made with flanged openings, then separate pieces will be made in separate molds. These would be doors, deck lids, hoods, grilles, floorpans, firewalls, dashes, etc. Some of these components will be single-skin, such as the dash, firewall, flooring, etc. Others will have a second component, such as the door inner structure and the deck lid inside piece. There has been some experimentation with foam coring of firewalls and floorpans, as well. In these designs, a second piece is made that will mate to the first unit, with a foamed core of polyvinyl chloride (PVC) between. This serves as a heat shield, but it seems a lot of extra work and expense for marginal improvement over traditional heat mats. The doors and deck lid may be a slightly thicker laminate than the body, for additional strength.

If an inner structure is to be molded, then laminated to the outer skin (door, deck lid, etc), it is best to leave the outer skin in the mold and fit the inner piece. Minor grinding or trimming may be needed for a perfect fit. You might need to add additional substructure to the outer skin prior to attaching the inner panel. Plan ahead.

If a 'glass floor has been created, it is usually installed to the body before the body is removed from the mold. This controls distortion. The firewall may have been molded as a part of the body, if not, it is usually installed to the body after the body has been removed from the mold. Metal floorboards and firewalls may be laminated to the fiberglass body, plywood floors and firewalls are common.

Once the body or part has completely cured, it may be removed from the mold. Small wooden wedges forced between the mold flanges will usually pop the two apart. If the parting agent is water soluble, warm water

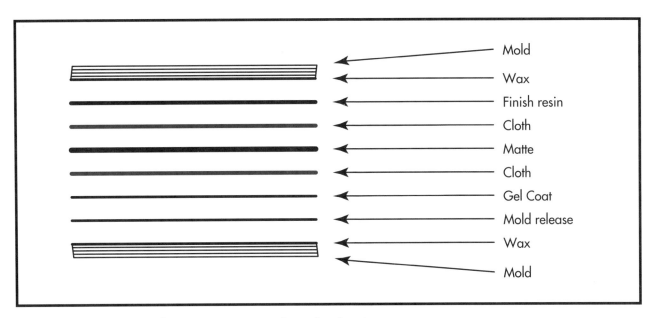

Mold
Wax
Finish resin
Cloth
Matte
Cloth
Gel Coat
Mold release
Wax
Mold

This is the sequence of events in a typical car body construction.

poured between the mold and body helps. Even compressed air can be directed between mold and body to get separation. Often a lot of popping and cracking noises are associated with removing a body from the mold, and plenty of prying pressure may be needed. Once the body is free of the mold, you will understand why you took the time and effort to make a female mold.

Just as it is vital to keep all your tools cleaned as you proceed, you'll need to clean the mold. If a water soluble parting agent was used, ordinary soap and water works nicely along with steel wool. If an acetate based parting agent was used, clean the mold with acetone. Just remember that acetone melts fiberglass, so get the mold surface dried and cleaned of the acetone right away. You only have a few minutes.

Don't destroy your molds. You may think they will never be used again, but time has a way of changing decisions. Turn the mold surfaces away from the sun and the elements, and they will last a very long time. You might even sell your molds for more than you have invested, as a way to recoup building costs.

ADDING SUBSTRUCTURES

MOUNTING FLANGES, HINGES AND WOOD OR METAL SKELETONS

There was a time in fiberglass car body history that the entire body was molded as a single unit, and when it was pulled from the mold that was it. The frame had some body support hoops in place, so the one-piece body could be bolted to the supports. Some contemporary race car bodies are still made this way where light weight is a factor, such as those for drag racing and to a limited extent sports car racing. For a street driven vehicle, however, strength is a major concern. So are doors, hoods, deck lids, fenders, etc. Government-mandated safety features are even involved. For a street driven vehicle, or one that gets tough off-road use, a substructure is

necessary for a molded fiberglass car body skin. The substructure creates the rigidity needed.

A full envelope body, a design with the front fenders and grille area molded as a unit with the main body, is fairly strong. A modular body which uses a separate hood and grille assembly, and separate fenders (primarily the older body styles) is also strong, but only in the body area. Both body types need the strength that comes from flooring and firewall, as well as other inner panels. Also, both types of bodies built today normally have some inherent support features as a part of the mold. These would be the door jambs and glass surrounds

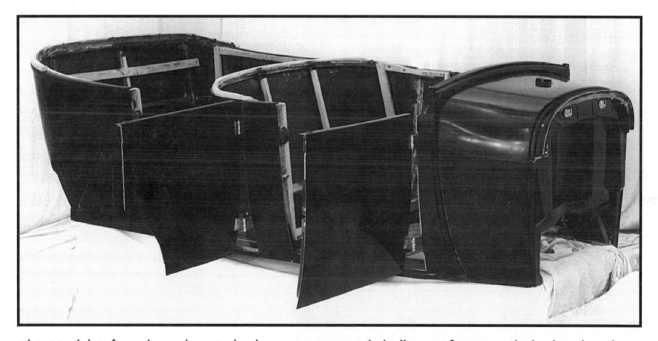

This Model A four-door phaeton body presents special challenges for strength, both in bending and in torsion. A set back firewall is made of fiberglass and laminated to the body, the flooring is flat with the bottom of the body, and the rest of the substructure is made of wood laminated to the fiberglass. The hinges bolt to wood substructures.

This fiberglass body is laminated to a steel subfloor, the one- by two-inch steel tube door jamb support is bolted to the frame and to wood substructure along top edge of body. The door jamb itself is made of steel laminated to fiberglass body. Epoxy works best for initial resin coat when attaching steel or wood to polyester resin body.

as well as gutter trays for the hood and deck lid. In addition, designers of production bodies and parts add extra fiberglass or stiffening in areas that have proven weak. Still, it is the added subassemblies (called substructures) that give a well-built fiberglass body outstanding strength.

The firewall is perhaps the first substructure added to a fresh body. Production bodies usually include a fiberglass firewall, these are normally available as original style or modified to popular shapes. If the engine is not original, or is relocated in the chassis (usually the case with a 'glass car) it may need additional firewall clearance. In at least one instance, a production fiberglass body uses a steel firewall (available stock or modified) as well as a steel floor.

The floor is usually the second substructure added, although it can be installed before the firewall, especially if it will be installed before the body is taken from the mold initially. Again,

production bodies may have fiberglass floors (pressure molds make floors smooth on both sides!), but for the sake of convenience and strength, floors are generally made of plywood or honeycomb composites.

If you have made a female mold that is accurate to within one-eighth inch, and you have trimmed the lower edge of the body very well, you should have a body that is "square" to the floor opening. Always use only new plywood, something made from a soft wood, and preferably made with waterproof glue. A hard wood does not bond well with normal resin. Plywood for flooring should be one-half- to three-quarter-inch thick, same for the firewall. Other bulkheads (such as behind the seat) can be three-eighth- to one-half-inch thick. If you want a very nice finish on the wood, get something that has been finish sanded on both sides.

Lay a flat sheet of plywood on the upturned body. If the lower body lip has been trimmed nicely, the plywood will

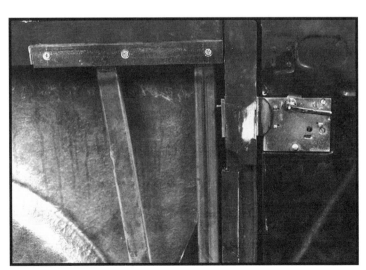

Steel and wood can be combined anywhere in a substructure, the door opening of a roadster or a convertible-type body must be extremely rigid.

Steel plates used anywhere on fiberglass body should be large enough to spread the load and should sandwich the fiberglass laminate.

hang down over the frame rails enough to cover the frame as viewed from the side. The Model A might have a floor nearly level with the body lower lip, leaving fully exposed frame rails. Set the body over the chassis, and align the rear wheels with the body. The frame rails should be perfectly level cross-chassis. Generally, the body is made level with the frame front-to-rear. If any special "rake" is desired (front of car lower than back, etc), this is done with suspension and tire sizes. Determine how the body will fit and block it into place at the desired height (relative to the frame).

Because the body is still flimsy, it is necessary to check it for square several times before 'glassing in the firewall or floor. Measure from the frame to the body at several points, front to rear. Measure diagonally at the firewall

lay flat in a few places. Sight down the flat sheet of plywood to make sure it truly is reasonably flat (no twisting front to rear). If the body is not to be "channeled" down over the frame, then the existing body lip is the shape that must be cut from the plywood. In practice, however, the flooring almost never fits the body at the body's lowest lip. For this reason, the homegrown fiberglass body should probably be set over the completed chassis before either the firewall or floor are added. Removed from the mold, the body will be wobbly, so handle with care and patience.

Whether the body is an envelope (such as a Cobra design) or modular (such as a Model A coupe) where you mount it on the chassis, height-wise, is vital to the car's eventual proportions. An envelope body will probably

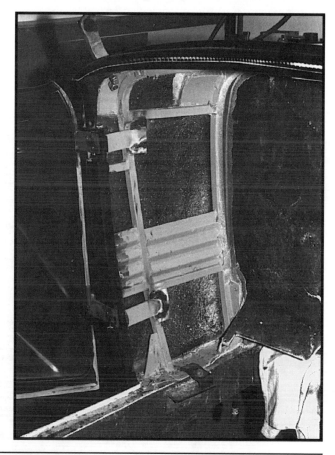

This is a tubing substructure Wescott uses on early Ford coupe bodies. The framework is made on a jig so it is exactly the same each time, and it is added to the fiberglass body while the body is still in the female mold. Note the steel extrusion panel in the sides, this anticipates federal regulations on safety.

opening and at the door jambs. If you want, you can make up some temporary angle brackets and fiberglass these to the body, then bolt the bracket to the frame. Or, you can be careful as you work and make cardboard patterns of the firewall opening and the floor shape. Since a car body tends to "belly out" as you get higher than the bottom lip, it will take several cut-and-try attempts to get a floor pattern that fits. The assumption is that the floor will be flat on the top of the frame.

Now is the time to say something about wood versus metal as a substructure material. Wood has a different expansion rate with temperature changes than does fiberglass. So does metal, but the difference is not quite as pronounced. Noting this, fiberglass boat builders often build in an expansion area where wood meets fiberglass at an acute angle. To do so, they leave a small air gap where the plywood edge would flush against the 'glass.

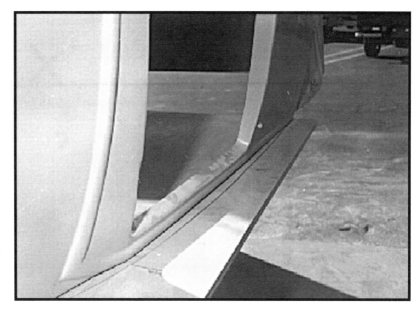

Thick plywood is usually the flooring of choice for homebuilders. The body is set on plywood and an outline of body is drawn in pen. In this case, there is a lip on the body inner side for the flooring to rest on.

They may use a piece of foam, or just leave it open. This is done to keep the plywood from eventually chaffing against the fiberglass and causing a stress point. Whether or not this is vital on a car body is subject for intense debate within the production community. For certain, on a very hot day and with light at a certain angle, it is possible to see lines in the body where wood is laminated to the inside. Of course, to a lesser degree you may also see where metal supports are laminated to the body.

If you are following this procedure to install the flooring, go directly from making the floor pattern to installing the firewall. Check the diagonal measurements again, making sure the body is

The flooring will be cut to fit the body, snugly in this case, then it is held temporarily in place with bolts. The body may be built without this convenient lip, plywood is bolted to frame and the body is positioned to correct the fit before 'glassing of the body to the floor.

In this case, the flat floor ends just ahead of the rear fenderwell, and resumes just aft. Narrow pieces of plywood are cut and clamped in place for fiberglassing over the frame rear kickup.

"square" on the chassis. If the cardboard pattern is an exact fit to the fiberglass opening where you want it to be, cut the plywood firewall and test it for fit. Whether you fit it tight or with a gap is up to you.

The wood is new, so it should be clean. You can sand where fiberglass will be applied, but some experts say this isn't entirely necessary. Still, roughing up the surface won't hurt, especially if polyester resin is to be used. Polyester resin does not bond to wood as well as epoxy. For this reason, some builders prefer to make the first bond between a body and wood with epoxy, then apply polyester over this. Other builders prefer to use a general purpose polyester resin and lap over onto the wood a couple of extra inches. Still others go ahead and make a full lay-up of fiberglass across

Narrow pieces of plywood may be held in place with duct tape during early mock-up, later they will be fiberglassed to each other and to the body.

Firewall may be put in at any time, but it is necessary that the body always be "square." Diagonal pieces of wood are added behind the seat area of this roadster. These can be temporary and removed at a later date when a plywood bulkhead is installed in the same area.

Thick wood is used for the substructure at the door flange. It is trimmed until it fits the body, then clamped in place while other pieces of framing are made.

either the top or bottom of the floor or back side of the firewall. While it is possible to fully encase wood with fiberglass, the argument is made that this then traps moisture in the wood.

At any rate, position the firewall and attach it to the body at four places with strips of resin saturated cloth. Lots of car builders use matte, or even roving, for these attachment laps, but cloth is far superior in strength. These initial tabs will hold the firewall in place while you check still again for alignment. When you are certain the firewall is exactly where you want it, 'glass the edges in place. A note here: A hard right angle in fiberglass is not as strong as a fillet. Some builders prefer to make the initial bond with fiberglass at a right angle (remember to sand the fiberglass body before applying the new 'glass), then building up a fillet with matte, and adding a final strip of cloth. You will probably do some cutting of the firewall for engine / transmission clearance, so leave finishing until last.

A rear door jamb wood upright is clamped to the fiberglass body, an angle strap keeps it in position on the floor.

A wood subassembly is made of several short lengths where the body curves around behind the seat. Again, these are trimmed to fit and held in place with clamps.

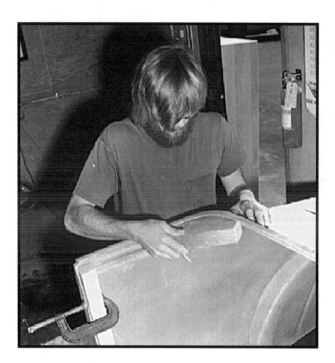

A large piece of block will be cut on a bandsaw to follow the narrow curve in a corner area.

The wood substructure is formed to fit dents in the fiberglass door flange.

Although a bandsaw makes cutting curves easier, a sabre saw will do the same job. This cowl door jamb upright is curved to fit the body, the reliefs are for two hinges and an opening limit strap.

With the firewall installed, the body will have gained considerable torsional rigidity. Cut the plywood flooring to the pattern. Use the largest piece of flat floor as possible, trimmed for clearance around the transmission, and bolted or clamped to the frame in two or three places. At the frame rear, a kick-up is common. This area can be formed from several narrow pieces of wood, installed after the main floor is 'glassed in place and cured.

Remove the body from the chassis, set the new floor in place, then set the body back in place. Get out your handy tape measure to be positive you are where you want to be. The floor should contour to the body nicely (with or without that air gap). Attach the floor with several strategically placed strips of saturated cloth, and measure again. If all is still exactly as you want, 'glass the floor to the body on the top side. After this kicks, finish the rear of the floor. You should now have a solid bottom all the way from the back lip of the body to the firewall. You may have needed some clearance holes here or there, or access holes. Remove the body, turn it upside down, and fiberglass between the body and the floor, lapping over the body up to three inches if possible, and five to six inches on the wood. Build up the joints with fillets if you want extra strength.

If bulkheads are to be added, such as between seat and trunk, many builders prefer to attach the plywood only along the floor and at several points along the top edge. They do not attach along the vertical body panels. If

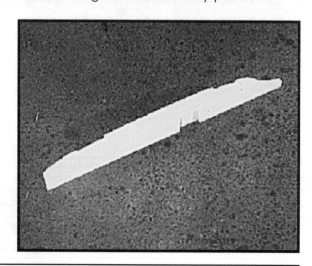

This is a fiberglass recessed firewall, as seen from the inside. Wood uprights on either side are mostly for mounting convenience of a cowl area substructure. Wood and metal should be laminated to fiberglass with an initial coating of epoxy resin, regular polyester resin can follow.

extra strength is wanted in the quarter panels, it is preferred to add laminates of 'glass to the body, or put in stiffeners.

Whether the body has the floor / firewall of metal, wood, or fiberglass, the overall strength of the "box" will be very similar. There should be no warping or deforming, but keep in mind that the body will continue to shrink. If you are not fully confident in your work, add all the body bolts to the floor and leave the unit to cure for several days. Go on a vacation, you have earned one at this stage.

There is occasion to use a fiberglass body without an attached floor, bulkheads, etc. In this case, the body skin is similar to an aluminum unit, wherein the skin attaches to a supporting framework which is considered a part of the chassis (framework which may or may not unbolt from the chassis). The body skin may be a single unit (as with drag racing Funny Car bodies), or it may be cut up into panels. Generally, this body is set over the chassis and aligned as we have explained. Square or round

metal tubing is then constructed to become interior formers. These will usually only approximate the body shape in cross section. These supports are often welded to the frame, then brackets are made between supports and body. Race cars often have the body attach at a pivot point (usually at the back) so the entire body can be tilted up for access. If this instant access is not vital, the body may be bolted at several points to supports. Sometimes, if the body is composed of several panels, these panels are held to the support brackets with aircraft Dzus fasteners. In this type of use, the body really has very little substructure, other than some brackets and a few stiffeners.

Substructures are places to bolt things as well as sources of extra body strength. This is where the decision to use either wood or metal, or a combination of both, comes into play. Some production manufacturers make a rather elaborate square tubing subassembly that is 'glassed into the body while the body is in the mold. This tubing normally attaches at the floor lip and high on the body (under the dash, under the rear window, etc), as well as at the

With the firewall in place, the cowl area substructure is pieced together. In addition to helping body strength, the wood serves as a mounting surface for interior upholstery panels.

door / hood / deck lid openings. It includes structure for the doors and deck lid, with attachment points for hinges. Such assemblies may look uncomplicated, but they are the result of considerable work, and production shops have jigs for them to speed construction.

It is not impossible for the homebuilder to

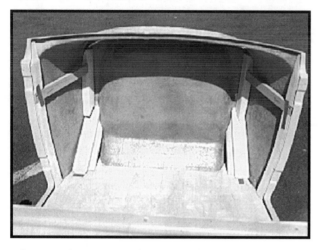

The weakest part of this cowl area is now the top of the dash lip, when the dash is installed that part becomes very strong as well.

If a recessed firewall is not used, the first substructure added between the floor and the flat firewall would be angled footboard supports. Flooring is cut out to clear the transmission, the firewall must be cut to clear bellhousing.

make up metal substructures, but any welding of the metal in proximity to the body should be done with extreme care since the fiberglass will burn readily. Usually, it works best to tack weld with a MIG welder, and finish weld with the framework away from the body. Thin walled one-half- and one-inch-square tubing is most commonly used. There are some square tubing benders in use by race car builders, gentle bends in square tubing can be done by hand. A tight radius bend in either round or square tubing can be done by filling the tube with sand, jamming wood pegs into either end, then heating the tube. The sand keeps the tube from collapsing.

When metal is being laminated to fiberglass, it should be clean and dry. Roughing up the surface with 80 grit sandpaper may help. As a rule, metal should be completely encapsulated by fiberglass for the best connection. In the case of brackets, it is possible to drill the metal plate full of holes to increase solidity of the attachment.

Wood is the more common substructure

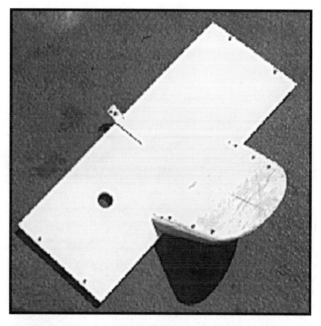

With the body on the chassis to make sure all clearance between engine / trans and floor / firewall is cut, a footboard may be made of plywood. This is usually made removable for later access to mechanicals.

The footboard is usually plywood, the transmission hump may be wood (as shown) or metal that screws to the wood.

material. While plywood is common for the floor, firewall, and bulkheads, other areas are generally made from thicker wood, trimmed to fit. Consider a typical one-piece body. In this case, the doors and deck lid will be cut from the body.

After the floor (and firewall if necessary) is installed, lengths of clear grain wood are laminated to the body where the openings will be. A piece of one-inch thick by eight-inch wide wood is set in the body at both sides of the door opening, running from the floor to the top body lip. Along the bottom line of the door, a piece of wood (usually about one by four inches) runs fore / aft between the vertical one by eights. These pieces of wood straddle the eventual door opening, on the inside. The wood is 'glassed to the body around the wood edges. Working from the outside, cut through the fiberglass body and the wood backing along the door outline. Use a premium blade, as the fiberglass will dull the blade quickly. Use care to get straight lines on the cut. With this single cut you have created both the door jamb on the body and the substructure in the door. Attach the exposed fiberglass edge to the wood with resin and cloth, and add or remove 'glass until the door opening is precise. Hinges and latch mechanisms attach to the wood substructure

easily, normally they are not fiberglassed unless they lap over to the body in some way.

In the event the body has been made with separate doors / deck / hood, with door jambs and flanges molded in place, additional wood may be added. In this case, lengths of wood from one to two inches wide (often shaped with a grinder to fit the body curvature) are cut to fit behind the flanges, on the door lips, etc. Production bodies have wood applied to these areas, the wood serves several functions. It is a tack strip for upholstery, it gives strength to the body, it is a mounting surface for hinges, latches, windshields, etc. As a rule, this wood is not totally encapsulated with fiberglass, and in some cases it is merely "glued" to the body with epoxy. An example of this epoxy would be Marine-Tex, the description on the can label tells it all. "Repairs damaged hulls in minutes, water-tight and stronger than before mishap. ... Repair leaks in fuel tanks, water tanks, piping,

When the flooring, firewall, and all other body substructure is in place, the body can be bolted to the chassis at all desired points. The result should be a combination that is perhaps stronger than a metal counterpart, it is definitely rugged.

If fiberglass flanges are to be made on the body prior to adding flooring, as a tooling convenience, bend a piece of cardboard as a backing.

food containers, cracks in engine crankcases and heads. … Bonds to most metals, plastics, hard and soft wood, plywood. … Impervious to oils, greases, fuel, brine, detergents and other chemicals. … "

Sometimes, the door / deck / hood is cut from the body before any wood has been 'glassed in place. After the part is cut out, the part and the body are returned to the mold. Wood or metal is placed on the body, overlapping the cut-out piece, this new "tray" is fiberglassed to the body, but not to the cut-

Tape this cardboard to the body, then use fiberglass cloth and resin to make a temporary flange. A similar cardboard support can be used for many molding problems.

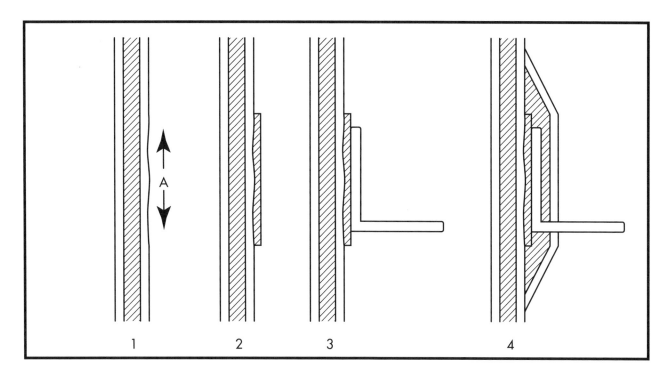

Metal brackets need to be thoroughly imbedded in a fiberglass wrap. The bare body is number 1. This is sanded, then a small piece of matte is laminated in place, 2. The metal bracket is positioned against the matte, 3, then more matte is used to cover the metal flange, 4. For best results, the metal bracket is installed using epoxy resin, the final coat can be polyester resin and fiberglass cloth. Epoxy resin takes a while to cure, this can be speeded by using heat lamps.

out. The cut-out piece now has something to set on. Something to stiffen the door / deck / hood is laminated to that cut-out piece. Or a core laminate may be included (more on that in a different chapter) to give more strength to the separate piece.

Making a body or part stiffer will be a matter of choice. For the average roadworthy vehicle body, weight is not a principle concern when it comes to a few pounds used to stiffen the body. Bulk will usually make the area stiffer, so matte or roving will probably be used as a straight laminate. Rough the body inner surface with sandpaper, wipe clean with acetone to get rid of any contamination, and brush on a coat of general purpose polyester resin. Lay the fiberglass on this, then saturate with resin, removing excess. Let this patch harden before adding a second layer. The final layer will be a non-tacky finish resin. The extra laminate thickness due to bulk makes the panel stiffer and stronger. Understand, however, that every

time and everywhere resin and fiberglass is added, some heat and distortion can be expected. This is usually·minimal, especially if you work with a thin laminate addition, letting each laminate kick before adding more. Repair of any distortion is done to the outside surface when preparing for paint.

Just as a bead can be rolled into a sheetmetal panel to gain rigidity, a roll or crown can be added to fiberglass. A length of metal or wood can be laminated to a panel. But fiberglass itself makes a good stiffening agent. Split a piece of plastic pipe and lay the open face on the panel, then lap fiberglass matte over this. Lay a length of garden hose or plastic tubing along the panel and overlay with fiberglass. This works very well around a lip where a rolled edge is needed, and if the hose or tubing is of PVC it will pull out of the cured tunnel. A piece of foam can be the core material. An interesting aside to use of the foam is that a large piece can be epoxy glued to the

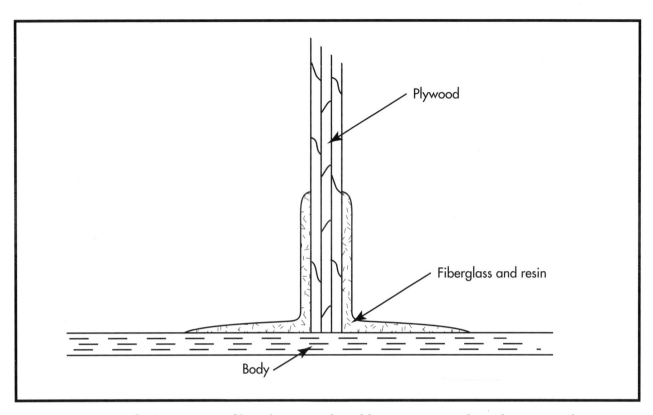

Plywood

Fiberglass and resin

Body

Wood can be set flush against a fiberglass panel and lamination made with resin and fiberglass. It is possible that a fiberglass panel will be weakened (over time) where it rubs against the wood.

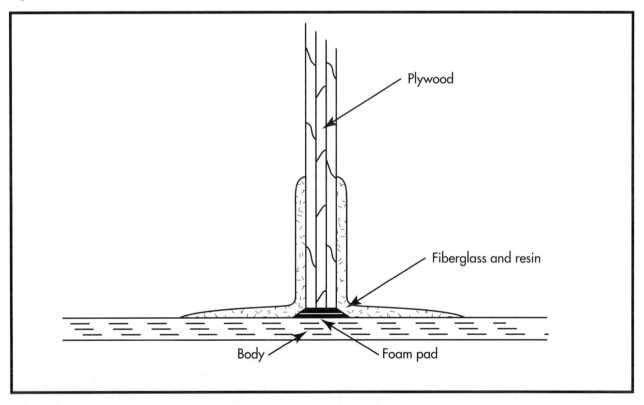

Plywood

Fiberglass and resin

Body

Foam pad

Some builders prefer to space wood away from a fiberglass panel, leaving an air gap or a foam pad between.

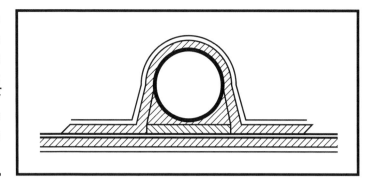

A fiberglass panel can be stiffened with a piece of thin-walled plastic tubing used as a form for a laminated 'glass tunnel. A garden hose coated with wax can be used, and the hose pulled out of the tunnel after the resin sets. The advantage of this approach is that the tunnel conforms to the panel curves.

fiberglass, the foam can then be sanded or carved into a shape, and fiberglass overlaid. A quick way to get a custom shape.

Sometimes weak areas will appear in the body design. On an open car, this is often on the cowl where the windshield will attach. For the sake of maximum strength, it usually works best to laminate a piece of metal plate on the cowl underside, through which the windshield frame bolts pass. Areas can be filled with matte, or bridged with foam and cloth. Each body and part must be treated differently in this respect.

Nothing can be bolted or screwed directly to fiberglass without some kind of attachment substructure. The bolt hole will wallow out immediately, the fiberglass will crush from the bolt torque, and the entire area around the bolt hole will deteriorate. If something is bolted to the fiberglass, that something will be one side of a sandwich. The substructure is the other side, so that the fiberglass is not harmed. Loads must be spread over a large area of laminate, and attachment points for hinges should be near flanges or highly curved panels (or on specially designed substructures).

On many antique era cars, such as the Model T Ford, door hinges are simple strap units (almost like a gate hinge). These are available from obsolete Ford parts houses.

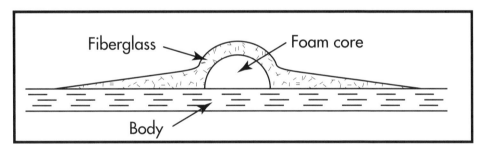

Fiberglass — Foam core — Body

A piece of foam can be split in half and molded to a panel to gain stiffness. The foam is left in place.

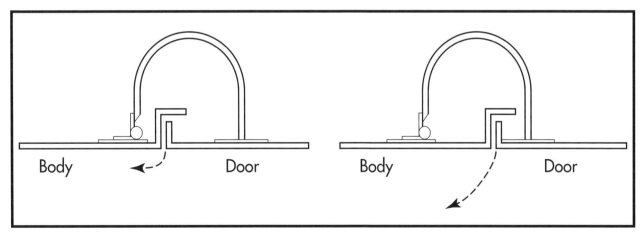

Body — Door   Body — Door

A hidden door or trunk hinge must have the hinge point well away from the door opening, otherwise the door will hit the body as it swings open.

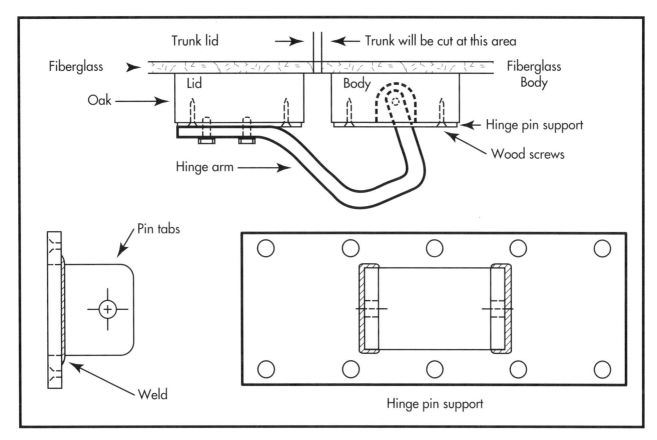

Hidden hinges are available from a number of aftermarket street rod suppliers, but they can be made of thick cold roll steel. Working out the pivot point so that panel swings free of body, opens fully, and settles back to body tight is the major design problem.

Hidden hinges appeared in the late 1940s, and they are very common on commercially available fiberglass hot rod bodies. They are available through street rod supply sources and work well on any style body design. Any hinge must be mounted securely to the substructure, whether it is wood or metal. The hidden hinge must have enough kick-out to the arm, and be mounted to both opening panel and body in such a way that the opening panel clears the body jamb area as the panel swings open.

A special note on hinges: It is imperative that all hinge pins on a panel align. A line drawn through one pin must go through the center of the other pin. One way to get this alignment is to remove the hinge pins and replace with a long length of threaded rod. Both hinges are held in alignment while they are attached to the substructure. Remove the threaded rod, add the pins.

The final type of substructure is a second laminate, such as the inner door panel or the inner deck lid panel. These panels usually have a great deal of surface irregularities designed in, to give them superior resistance to warping or bending. When these inner panels are attached to the body skin, the result is a lightweight but very strong combination, in either metal or fiberglass. Many production bodies come with these inner structures. The inner panel is laminated to the outer skin while the outer skin is in the female mold. If there will be another substructure between these two panels, either metal tubing or wood, that is installed before the inner panel is put in place. In a door, this would be the substructure mounting for the hinges and the door latch mechanism. These panels may be overlooked by the homebuilder, but they are almost industry standard in production lines.

CORES FOR FIBERGLASS LAMINATES

Fiberglass construction has been around for a long time now, time enough for engineers to figure countless ways to use it. Also long enough to figure how to make it extremely strong. Interestingly, until recent years most of the advancing technology has been limited to the aerospace industry. Off and on major automotive manufacturers have touched on these advances, while amateur car builders have hardly any knowledge of the techniques. At the same time, aircraft homebuilders have been using the technology for decades.

Car enthusiasts often mistakingly call this composite fiberglass. In fact, anything that is composed of more than one element would be a composite. Thus, a typical fiberglass body or fender would be a composite. The fiberglass laminate may be located between a wood or metal substructure and some outside piece, such as a windshield post. This would be a form of sandwich, with the 'glass as the central element. However, if a fiberglass laminate is on either side of a core material, the result is also a sandwich. A sandwich that can make a dramatic difference in fiberglass panel strength.

The key is in the sandwich core. This core can be anything. When a wood or metal substructure has a layer of fiberglass on either side, such as a plywood floor, the combined unit is much stronger than the individual components. But, the real advantage of sandwich core construction is in gaining great

strength with only a small increase in component weight. This would be vital on a homebuilt airplane, but the weight factor is less important on a car body. Of greater concern is the improvement in strength.

Suppose a car deck lid or hood is the typical laminate of fiberglass cloth / matte / roving. Give that component a strength factor of I. Split that laminate thickness, one-half to each of two pieces. Now, add a core material such as foam or honeycomb between the two, and glue each fiberglass laminate to the core with epoxy. With almost the same weight as the original piece of laminate, the strength has been increased by a factor of about 3. The stiffness is increased by a factor of nearly 7. Double the core thickness and the strength increases 9 times and the stiffness is up by about 37. A really good example of this is foam core posterboard, from your local art supply. A foam sheet about one-eighth-inch thick (which is easily broken) is sandwiched between two very flimsy pieces of posterboard. Individually, they have very little stiffness or strength. As a sandwich, this foam core board is very stiff and reasonably strong.

A number of core materials are used. In wood, the most common is balsa, followed by pine, redwood, fir, mahogany, spruce, etc. The weight of the wood and its compressibility are major factors in a decision to use a wood core. As a rule, wood (other than a substructure frame) will not be used in making a car body. Foam core material may be polystyrene, polyurethane, polyvinyl chloride, polymethacrylimide, polyimide, and syntactic. Honeycomb cores may be anything from paper to metal. The cost of these materials is all over the chart, but sometimes the more expensive aircraft materials are available in small quantities via surplus outlets. A rule of thumb is that the heavier the material, the higher the cost.

Fortunately, for the car builder, common construction type foam works nicely. Although a few specialty aircraft use Polystyrene (commonly known as Styrofoam), it is soluble in polyester and vinyl ester resins, and will soften in petroleum products. At the lumber yard, you'll find it in a light blue color. It also is made in a bead form, which is really not satisfactory for sandwich strength. This stuff can be used if you are very careful, but it isn't the best selection.

Polyurethane foams come in a huge variety, but only a very few are really usable. Clark foam (bright white) is strong, Last-A-Foam is light brown. Most urethane foams are based on a polyether formula and resist solvents, but they give off extremely poisonous gas when burning. All but Last-A-Foam burn readily! Mix this with the flammability of fiberglass and you see a problem. Some urethane is available as a foam-in-place convenience, this doesn't work for the homebuilder. Best advice is to avoid polyurethane foams.

PVC (polyvinyl chloride) comes in sheets, it is not completely resistant to solvents, but it ranks with the urethanes in many areas. Better than the PVC or the urethane is polymeth-acrylimide (sold as Rohacell), bright white in color, it is considered one of the best foams for fiberglass cores. It is also more expensive. A neat foam is trade named Imitech, it is a polyimide and it will not burn! It is plenty lightweight for car bodies, and it might be considered for firewalls and bulkheads surrounding in-body gas tanks.

You can make your own foam by mixing micro-balloons with resin. You get the micro-balloons at the fiberglass supply source Make sure the balloons are compatible with the resin. The strength of the foam depends on the materials used. In the case of a car body or part, this is not a major factor. Neat thing about this kind of foam is that you can use it as a foam-in-place solution. This is called a syntactic foam.

A honeycomb core is made of metal, paper, or woven fabric, and is generally hexagon in cell shape. Most of these honeycombs are coated with resin, which increases its strength, but also produces rigidity. Some flexibility in a honeycomb core is needed to conform to a slightly curved car body panel, if great flexibility is needed Nomex is the style to use. Kraft paper honeycombs tend to absorb a great deal of humidity, and lose strength, so most builders avoid the type. Nomex Aramid paper honeycombs are available, these are very common in the aircraft industry, and are appearing in some really advanced limited production car bodies. Korex Aramid, which includes Kevlar fibers, is a new honeycomb that is very expensive. There are also some really exotic honeycomb cores, but for a typical car body the less expensive types work very well. It should be noted that there is some technology afoot for using foam and honeycomb cores sandwiched between metal on one side and fiberglass on the other. This is in some very complicated car body designs, but its use is extremely limited, and very expensive. It is not for the homebuilder, obviously.

If foam has to be cut, a serrated bread knife works fine. So does a very sharp knife, and a router can be used to make rounded edges. A bandsaw or regular table saw will cut foam, and shaping is done easily with sandpaper on a sanding block. If two or more pieces of foam are to be used in a sandwich, be sure the pieces are glued together. If not, the seam is a weak spot waiting to fracture.

"One reason I bought my 5-window body from Flatlander's is, it's even got the original drip rails!"

— Clyde Roberts, Dolomite, Alabama

FLATLANDER'S 1932 Ford Chopped 5-window coupe features working or filled cowl, recessed stock style firewall, full floor, working windows in doors, 2 dashboard styles, hinged and latched doors, garnish moldings, latched remote opening trunk lid. *Also:* our custom-built steel interior skeleton with reinforced cowl area, built-in column support, seat belt mounting brackets, and more. Doors are reinforced with steel for rigidity and structural support. The fiberglass body is hand laid black gel coat with layers of 1½ oz. fiberglass cloth and CORMAT® for extra strength. *Now in stock, $5450.*

FLATLANDER'S also makes a great traditional "Deuce" roadster. The body is built from hand laid reinforced fiberglass with recessed factory-style firewall, filled or working cowl vent,

factory-style door hinges, latched deck lid, and full floor. It uses the same style inner steel structure as in FLATLANDER'S '32 5-window. Now, lots of shops sell "Deuce" roadsters, *but not like this one!* **Our mold was made from an original steel Ford roadster, not knocked-off from someone else's fiberglass body.** Check it out – *introductory offer $3932!*

Special "Project '32" Body plus Chassis Combo Price! Combine our 5-window coupe body and our "Project '32" Deuce chassis *(above, $4932)* and get the fitted package for *only $9832...* or Roadster plus Chassis, *only $8832.*

If you've always loved "Graffiti" coupes like we have, call us! We'll have the parts for *your* "Graffiti" project, or we can build one for you!

CALL FLATLANDER'S for all your hot rodding needs. Everything from repair to your turnkey dream rod... all the parts from an axle to a complete chassis, from the radiator to the rear end – just call us! *Our answers are still FREE.* Call 804-440-1932, and ask for Alan or Dave. **FLATLANDER'S.** *We're Still The One!*

FLATLANDER'S HOT RODS, INC. for Traditional / Nostalgic Bodies, Chassis, Components & Cars
1005 W. 45th St., Norfolk, VA 23508 • 804-440-1932, Fax 423-8601 • *REAL HOT RODS, NOT KIT CARS!* • Catalog $3 refundable with purchase.

Foam or honeycomb can be used on the underside of a hood, inside doors, and under a deck lid. It can also be attached to any body panel where additional strength is needed. Carve or sand the foam to fit the panel shape, it will bend only slightly to conform. Honeycomb is usually flexible enough for the typical body compound curves, but you'll need a very open honeycomb for tight curves. Apply a coat of resin to the fiberglass panel, set the foam or honeycomb in place, and then wait for the resin to kick. A laminate of fiberglass cloth can be applied to the exposed foam face, and the sandwich is done. If honeycomb is used, the cells can get a dose of resin (don't use much), then the top layer of fiberglass applied. If the honeycomb cells are really open, the 'glass may try to sag in each hole.

The advantage of this type of core sandwich is in making body panels very strong yet light in weight. The core material will also act as a sound deadener and insulation. Something to consider for a roof area, a firewall, or a floor.

FIBERGLASS ADHESIVES

GLUING THE FIBERGLASS CAR TOGETHER

Actually, it is probably more correct to simply say adhesives, since chemical bonders have been developed to the stage where most every material can be glued permanently to another material. In this respect, more and more new production line automobiles are using glued structures. Sometimes this is just plastic to plastic, but it can be plastic to metal, metal or plastic to window glass, etc. Although resin bonding may seem high tech and new, this technology is a direct transfer from the aircraft industry. It started to gain momentum in the late 1940s. Pioneer adhesives were generally phenol-resorcinol based, and they are now joined by Cyanoacrylate (model airplane builders love this stuff), Anaerobic (Locktite thread locking compound is an excellent example), and a long list of common and exotic epoxies. Even polyester and vinyl ester resins can be adhesives.

The more common hardware store adhesives are wood glues that work okay around the house but don't really do the job for the wood, plastic, glass, or metal used on a car body. Cyanoacrylate and Anaerobic adhesives are very expensive, so for practical purposes they are out. This leaves epoxies and vinyl esters as the best glues for our purposes. But, and this can be important, those shrink-pack epoxies at the hardware store aren't always what you need. A plastic supply store will have quality adhesives, as will most marine supply stores. You can also get good adhesives at an automotive paint supplier, the kind used for installation of newer automobile plastic bumpers, body panels, and fenders. These new urethane "glues" are two-part, expensive, and kick very fast. Most go off in about 30 seconds on a warm day, if you are lucky you get three or four minutes on a cold day. They are available in rigid, semi-rigid, and flexible varieties.

A variety of adhesives areavailable, some are very thin and some thick as putty. The very thin can be useful when you are working with two mating surfaces that are very flat, but if too much adhesive is squeezed out of the joint the strength will be low. If thin adhesive is used on parts that do not have closely matched mating

The advantages of using polymer adhesives are a quick setting time, no problem with contaminants after curing, compatability with metal as well as fiberglass car parts, and they are excellent with all woods. This wooden seat structure has been saturated with a very thin urethane and will be glued in place.

Many adhesives can have any kind of inert material added as a filler, this is sawdust over a rotted wood connection. The filler is sanded, a thin coat of polyester resin applied, and it is ready for paint.

surfaces, there is not enough "fill" and the result is little or no joining. A small bit of filler in very thin adhesive often helps the bond, an adhesive that has a putty consistency is advisable where you need to fill lots of gaps. When two pieces of fiberglass are being bonded, such as an inner substructure and an outer skin, it is usually the practice to use a vinyl ester putty-consistency adhesive. This sets in a reasonable time, and has excellent gap-filling properties.

One interesting urethane adhesive is directed right at the specialty car market. Known as RSP, it is mixed 1:1 and will set in about three minutes at 70 degrees. Increase the temperature and it sets faster, chill the components in ice and it takes longer to kick. This chemical has the viscosity of water, but it can be made into a paste of any consistency by adding any kind of filler, from sawdust to ordinary dirt to metal shavings to cement.

Mixed plain, it glues two materials together with or without pressure. Two very smooth surfaces to be glued will bond better if a tiny amount of talc powder is added to make sure there is minimum "squeeze out" of RSP at the joint. Because of the viscosity, RSP penetrates rotten wood immediately, and it can be nailed or threaded within minutes. So, many car restorers use RSP to make poor wood strong. Then, by mixing it into a thick paste with wood sawdust, it becomes a workable filler for the same wood surface. Since any kind of inert material can be the filler, RSP can be use as a workable filler on plastic and metal as well.

An interesting attribute of RSP is that it makes an excellent casting resin. It reproduces mold surface features remarkably well. Car builders use it for making dash knobs, using an available knob as the male buck for a silicone female mold. Then a mixture of RSP and talc powder (which can be tinted with any dry pigment) is poured into the mold. Instant knob.

New adhesives appear constantly, which is an excellent reason to become a frequent visitor to the plastic supplier in your area.

FITTING PARTS

MAKING ALL THE PIECES FIT AND WORK AS THEY SHOULD

After a body, or a complicated part, has been molded, it is not very rigid. Adding a substructure (sub assembly) to the unit makes the body or part very strong. This additional work will have been performed, for the most part, with the body still in the mold (although the body may have been removed from the mold temporarily), as a means of alignment and controlling any distortion.

The laminate will probably still have some rough edges to trim. A saw or cut-off wheel is needed for major surgery, since the resin has long since cured. Once the major excess is trimmed, a hand file and / or grinding disc will do the finish work. Wear a mask and protective clothing, because the fiberglass dust will be everywhere. The smooth outside surface should be cleaned of any remaining parting agent, using acetone and steel wool for stubborn residue (water and soap for water soluble parting agent).

The body should now be bolted to the chassis. Obviously, this chassis must be correct

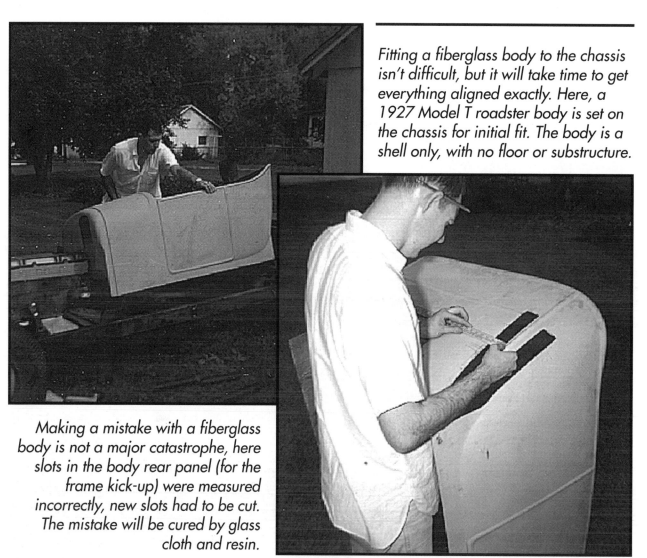

Fitting a fiberglass body to the chassis isn't difficult, but it will take time to get everything aligned exactly. Here, a 1927 Model T roadster body is set on the chassis for initial fit. The body is a shell only, with no floor or substructure.

Making a mistake with a fiberglass body is not a major catastrophe, here slots in the body rear panel (for the frame kick-up) were measured incorrectly, new slots had to be cut. The mistake will be cured by glass cloth and resin.

A builder cuts clearance for the driveshaft in the back of the body. This ease of making changes during fitting is a major advantage of building with fiberglass over metal.

correct fit of component parts, particularly with an open body. If, during construction, the body has warped a slight amount, it will usually pull into alignment on a straight frame.

When the body is placed on the frame, with no body bolts installed, check for warping. This will show as one side of the body-to-frame alignment will be different from the other side. If there is a slight deviation, check the floor-to-frame clearances. If the floor fits flush with the frame, but you detect some warping, perhaps the floor has been installed to the body off kilter. The solution is a thicker body washer(s) in one area to gain alignment. If the body is in alignment, but the floor-to-frame clearances are askew, the same washer (or body mounting welt) treatment is the cure. Do

in all phases of alignment, especially relative to twist. Do not plan on using a lot of shims between body and chassis to cure a twisted or badly bent frame. Once a chassis is on the road, a small amount of twist and frame distortion is possible, when assembling the car start with a true frame. This is vital to getting

Closed bodies are stronger than open bodies, and heavier. Once the body is set on the chassis, holes are drilled in the floor and the body is bolted in place. Some commercial fiberglass bodies come with these holes pre-drilled, providing a guide for holes in the frame.

The T body sets down over the tubing frame four inches, the body can be blocked temporarily in place while the plywood floor is shaped and installed. With this type of body, the wood or metal substructure can be added and doors cut open with the body bolted to the frame.

Once the plywood floor is installed and 'glassed securely to the body, the firewall and footboard can be installed. A hole is cut in the footboard for pedal(s), another for the steering shaft.

not mount fiberglass laminate directly to the frame! Always have an interface of some kind. While fiberglass is strong, it is very susceptible to abrasion.

A closed car body is really just a box, and as such is a strong structure. For this reason such a body will usually have a very good initial fit of doors and deck lid (and hood, if it is an envelope body). When such a body is bolted to a chassis, the combination becomes even stronger, particularly if the body has opening flanges molded in and all substructure in place. Doors can be set into place temporarily, and hinge locations marked. If a metal substructure is used, the hinges are attached by bolts. If a wood substructure is used, or a combination of wood and metal, the hinges can be attached by… bolts. Do not use

wood screws to attach hinges to wood. The door is heavy, and it will eventually pull wood screws loose. It is likely that some trimming of fiberglass and wood will be needed to get the hinges exact, check carefully for hinge bind and make certain that any combination of hinges have the hinge pins in alignment. It is a rare instance when the hinge is molded to the body or door / deck lid, usually some sort of attachment point is molded to the fiberglass body or part. If a hidden hinge is used on a deck lid, one part of the hinge is usually attached to the deck lid (a temporary attachment during fitting), the lid is installed on the body and aligned, then the hinge part for the body is temporarily attached. This may be done by having metal or wood attachment points mounted to the hinge, then placing this attachment against the body and laminating it in place with cloth and resin.

Despite all the pre-planning, it is sometimes necessary to make changes, such as this cut-out in the trunk area of a Model A body, needed to clear the coil-shock suspension. A new cover can be made of fiberglass, using a cardboard mold.

One of the problem areas of fitting a fiberglass body is always the clearance at firewall and transmission. The tighter the firewall opening around the transmission, the greater the foot room, but this requires some extra work in designing the footboard. Here a flat footboard will be used, lots of foot room is lost. Note that the firewall is fiberglass.

When trying to get an excellent fit between fiberglass doors and the body, it is possible to add fiberglass or epoxy to the edge of either the door or the door post, whichever is not straight. The gap in this case is caused by slight shrinkage of both the door and the post.

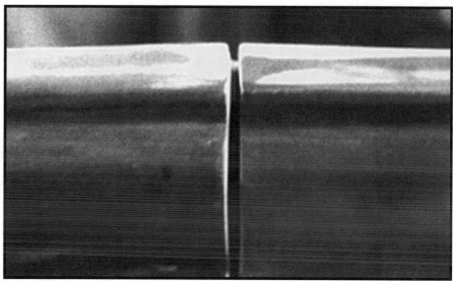

Again, all this should be temporary, until the deck lid has been checked for correct operation, then final fiberglassing can be done.

On an open body, it is often necessary to get door alignment exact by shimming the body. These shim points will be between frame and floor at the rear door post, the front door post, and the firewall. With a four-door phaeton body, add a shim point at the rear of the rear door opening.

Making an adjustment at any one of these points on an open car will affect the opposite side's alignment.

Early model car bodies were notorious for being unequal, side to side. Factory workers made on the spot adjustments, so fit of various panels was often haphazard. This should not be the case of a fiberglass body that has come from a really good buck / mold. Door openings on a good body should be identical, deck lid

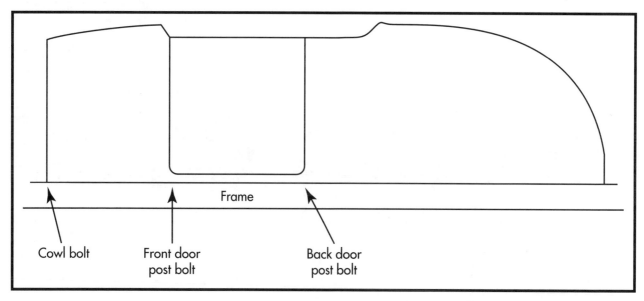

Frame

Cowl bolt   Front door   Back door
              post bolt   post bolt

Door adjustment points on all modular bodies are at the cowl / firewall, the front door post, and the rear door post. By increasing thickness of shims at these points the door alignment can be set almost perfectly. On a four-door touring body, the additional adjustment is at the rear door, rear post. A small amount of shimming makes a great difference in door fit. Closed bodies normally require no shims for door fit, full envelope bodies (sports car types) that are open can have some adjustment for doors but not as much as the antique body styles.

It is possible to mix and match fiberglass parts more easily than with metal, here a 1932 Ford custom dashboard is mated to a Model A body. At either side of the dash, fiberglass will be fashioned to fill large areas so that the body fits the dash. Cardboard can be positioned as a backing when making such fiberglass fillers, to hold the resin and cloth in place, then the cardboard is discarded. A thicker viscosity resin is useful when working on vertical or overhead lay-up.

opening should be true, etc. Thus, a separately molded door or deck lid should fit the opening with an excellent clearance all around the opening. If this is not the case, the door or the opening can be modified by adding resin and glass, or by using one of the quick-setting vinyl ester putties. In this respect, the fiberglass body or part is much easier to fit exactly than a metal body.

Once the doors and deck lid are positioned exactly, with hinges in place, the latch mechanism can be installed.

It is not uncommon for a door or deck lid panel to flatten slightly during all this work. This should be only a tiny distortion, easily cured with ordinary

Almost always fenders and small parts will have just enough warp and shrinkage to cause misalignment during assembly. The parts need to be bolted in place, which puts them in the correct location for any given chassis or body location, then 'glass or polymer putty is used to make all the mating surfaces agree.

Once metal is given a certain shape, it tends to stay there. Fiberglass will continue to shrink and distort until it is bolted in place, then (over time) it reshapes to the stress of location. Note here how the grille splash apron does not fit with the fender, even with both pieces bolted in place. Make corrections to the easiest piece, probably the fender lip in this case.

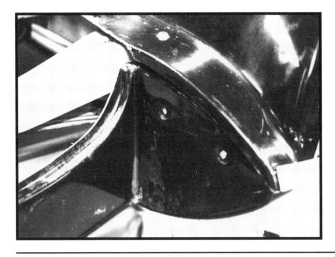

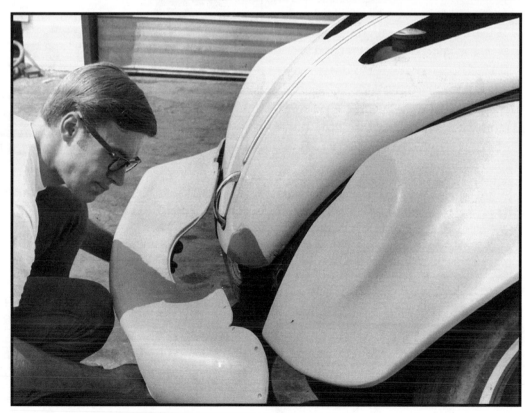

Sometimes a part is purposefully made larger than needed, it must then be trimmed to fit. This front fender splash apron for a 1934 Ford is cut to size using a cut-off wheel.

fiberglass filler. If there is a drastic panel discrepancy, expect to add a layer or more of new glass and lots of hand labor to get the panel back into shape.

If there is any remaining substructure to be added to the body, now is the time to do it.

The splash apron is set in place for a trial fit with grille shell and frame. If the part is trimmed too much, it can be repaired with 'glass.

No matter how well a mold has been constructed, individual fiberglass parts will probably not be a bolt-up without some tweaking, bolt everything together and make marks with a felt tip pen where extra trimming or additions must be made.

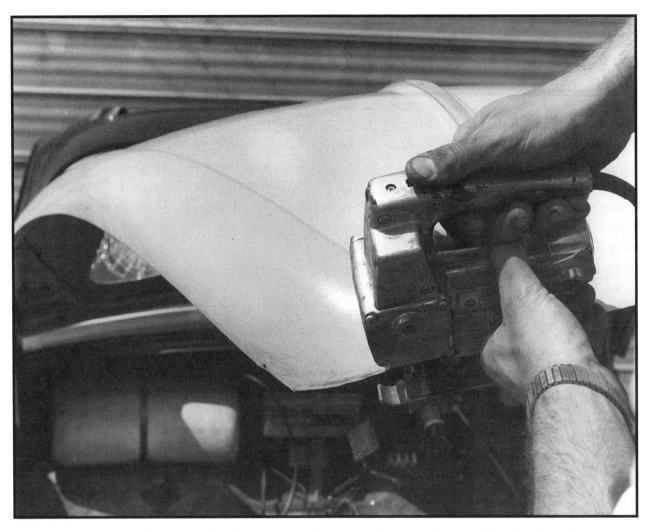

The edge of a VW fiberglass hood is trimmed with a saber saw for excellent fit, the edge must be sanded to a smooth finish prior to painting.

The body is in place, the doors and other panels are added, so all alignment should be complete. Door glass mechanism is added at this time, coupe roll-up rear windows are added, just about everything is done to the body or part to make it complete.

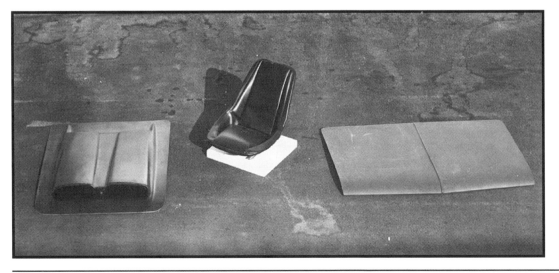

Fiberglass parts can be made for just about any part of the automobile body, even seats are of 'glass.

Fiberglass body parts are a quick way to reduce weight of a factory car, usually this is for competition purposes, but as a body style gets older, metal becomes harder to find. Some companies make parts, some homebuilders make their own parts. Fitting these 'glass parts takes a bit of time, but with the new polymer adhesives the fiberglass addition is merely a matter of gluing to a metal base. All of these parts were for drag racing, weighing about 100 pounds versus 500 pounds for metal.

Typical of the shrinking problems of fiberglass is the cowl top on the Model T body. It will often sag, requiring additional resin and fiberglass as well as plastic filler to make it level and smooth. In the cowl top corners, where the windshield posts fit, it is usually necessary to build up the corners with resin saturated glass, then setting the windshield posts in place while the fiberglass laminate kicks. Vaseline is a good small-area release agent, keeping the metal posts from bonding.

Metal parts used with a modular body, such as this hood, must be in place when fiberglass panels are being fit. The fiberglass is where all the trimming and adding is normally done to make pieces fit metal components.

This is also the time to do any custom changes to the body or part that could not be accomplished at the mold phase. This may include adding parts with adhesive, molding them to the body, or checking the fit of bolt-on parts (the latter will be removed for paint).

This is when fenders are carefully checked for fit, the edges smoothed, etc.

Go over the entire body very carefully. Look for any kind of discrepancy, particularly any air bubbles. Puncture the bubbles, clean the area, and add filler. Large bubbles should be trimmed and a mixture of resin / fiberglass strands used for repairs. Once the entire body has been checked and blemishes repaired, and all the panels adjusted for fit, the body can be sanded and given an initial coat of primer. Except for very minor adjustment, no more parts fitting should be required.

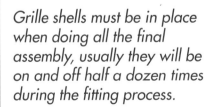

Grille shells must be in place when doing all the final assembly, usually they will be on and off half a dozen times during the fitting process.

Fenders almost always need to be tweaked to get a proper fit, once bolted in place let the body set in a warm shop, or the hot sun, and these parts will settle into shape.

FINISHING FIBERGLASS

At this point, the fiberglass body or part is ready to finish, as in applying paint, upholstery, wiring, etc. We are concerned only with getting to the point of spraying the final coats of paint. Doing the paint and additional work is the same as with any car, thus the subject of other books (our own *How To Do Electrical Systems* will be invaluable in this respect).

All of the adjusting of parts has been accomplished. If the car has any metal panels that must be made, such as hoods for old body styles, or bumper brackets, etc, these should be fabricated during the fitting parts phase.

The edges of fiberglass can be cruel to flesh, which is a good reason to file and sand every exposed edge. The inner surfaces will be rough, in most cases the only alteration might be a light sanding and some paint. Do not add underseal, as this is nearly impossible to remove if future repair or customizing is undertaken.

The assumption is that the fiberglass has not been laminated with a color pigment in the gel coat. Colored bodies have been available through the years from manufacturers, especially dune buggy bodies, but the finish is seldom of the quality most homebuilders want.

Once again, go over the entire car very carefully, looking for tiny air bubbles or craze / fracture lines in the surface. At this point, all repairs will be similar to any preparation, metal or fiberglass, except that the fiberglass body or part can only be repaired with fiberglass. Chances are very good that the body, or parts with large surfaces, will not be as perfect as desired. This will require special attention.

Thoroughly clean the surface with regular pre-paint wax and grease remover. Sand the

The underside of the floor, and all the inside surfaces of the fiberglass body, can be sprayed with paint. This helps to seal the fiberglass and eliminate the "fresh" fiberglass look. Mask off the outside surface to prevent overspray.

fiberglass surface with a rough sandpaper, 35-grit is okay if you do not use enough pressure to sand through the surface resin, on out-of-view areas such a door flanges you can use 80-grit. Use a finer grit paper if the coarse grit makes you nervous, but plan on a bunch of sanding. If you do sand through the gel coat, repair it with gel coat. Thoroughly clean the surface again, and inspect to make sure that every inch of the shiny surface has been sanded.

Spray on a good coat of two-part sealer. Neat thing about this sealer is that a plastic filler can be applied directly over the sealer. For outstanding end results in the paint job, use a quality two-part acrylic urethane primer next. Once the primer is dry, use rattle-can lacquer (black works good) for a guide coat. Stand back from the surface about two feet, and spray the lacquer on "dry." This should be a thin, blotchy skim coat of paint.

From here on, wet sand only. The idea of the paint guide coat is to help make the surface as smooth as possible, with no waves or distortions, because they will show in the final paint job. Various block sanding techniques have been developed through the years, one of the most effective is to wrap a sheet of 240-grit wet grade sandpaper around an ordinary paint mixing stick. This stick is about a foot long, an inch or so wide, and thinner than a yardstick, which makes it flexible. Run this "block" over the surface, and low spots in the primer will still show the black lacquer. Block sand the high spots and repeat the guide coat process, if you had a really good female mold you may still have to block sand the body or part five or six times, maybe more. For areas where the paint stick will not fit, use a regular six-inch rubber sanding block. When you block sand the surface and all of the guide coat paint sands off, you have a smooth panel. After each block sanding session, clean the surface thoroughly. The final sanding will be with 400-grit sandpaper on a 3M hand-sanding pad, contrary to old-timer tales, this final sanding is done in a circular motion on the larger panels.

Clean all the sanding residue from the body or part, and you are ready for the final paint.

WINDSHIELDS, SIDE GLASS, ETC.

ADDING THE KIND OF GLASS FOR SEEING THROUGH

There are two types of safety glass used in specialty car construction, flat and curved. When building your own fiberglass car, flat glass can be a part of the design. This can be for door glass, rear window, and windshield. Curved glass can also be for front, side, and rear. It is up to you what will be used, but wisdom always dictates selecting glass that is already available (and likely to be available in the future). A tour through the local auto wrecking yard will yield considerable glass options for a specialty car.

Flat safety glass is the easiest to cut, is available in a variety of tints, and is the least expensive. Unfortunately, it is not compatible with many special body designs. For instance, while flat glass may be desirable on the older production body styles (up through the early 1950s), it seldom works really well with a modern design. In a closed car with a body shape that is highly rounded, a flat side or rear glass is a major break in the design flow. You can work around the problem, but it will always be there. On an open car, this isn't quite

Installation of a windshield in any closed fiberglass car will be similar to the installation of this flat glass in a Poli-Form 1934 Ford coupe. Flush mounting windshields has replaced mounting with the use of the original windshield frames. Start your installation by making a cardboard pattern for the glass and having a local shop cut approved safety glass. Test the fit of the glass.

The depression for a windshield will probably be deep enough to accept a metal frame. When flush mounting the glass use soft rubber blocks to space the windshield away from the back flange and to bring the glass flush with the front of the opening. Use small blocks at base of the opening to get perimeter spacing, and remove these blocks before adding final trim.

The windshield can be held in place with urethane, but it is reported that this product breaks down after prolonged exposure to the sun, which is why factories paint the edge of the glass black. Apply a coat of urethane around the glass opening, where the glass contacts the edge.

the major problem, since there are many curved windshields available, and the two-piece "motor boat" style windshield seems to be adaptable to most body shapes. These are the famous "DuVal" windshields that are being produced again, you can locate them through any street rodding magazine. They are already low enough in height to seem chopped, and they fit at a rakish angle.

When trying to find a stock windshield for a special body, the width is the first consideration. It seems that most homebuilt cars end up with a width that is approximately that of

Run a thin coat of urethane around the edge of the windshield. This coat of urethane will mate with the line of urethane on the body opening. Use care, once the glass is in place the urethane sets fast and no further adjustment of the glass is possible.

Windshield surround rubbers are common items now. The thin molding from S-10 Blazers is popular. The angle of the lower corners of the windshield were marked off on a pattern for convenience, and the ends of the rubber trimmed to match.

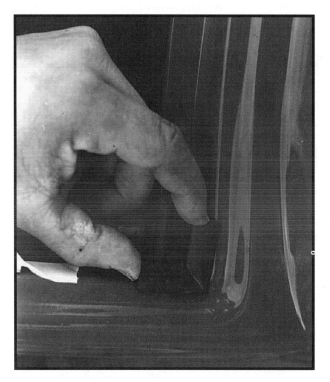

Two test pieces of rubber molding are set into the body cavity to make sure the angles fit.

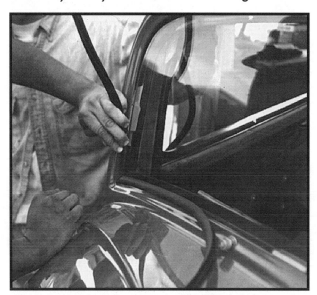

One end of the rubber molding is cut on angle, then the molding is tucked into place around the glass edge. This molding fits between body and glass, but it does not hold the glass in place, that is the function of the urethane adhesive.

The lower piece of molding is cut to fit. It is best to cut slightly long and trim as needed to get a final tight fit.

a compact or mid-size production car, since the chassis involved will have about the same tire track as a modern car. For a closed-coupe sports car-type body, the windshield variety is very diverse. For an open car, something that will have a curved glass with either angled sides or dog-leg sides, the options are more limited. An open car generally has a lower windshield height. Production convertibles and a very few closed-body styles have the low windshields, it is worth taking extra time to find such a windscreen. Cutting curved windshields is not impossible, but it may take some searching to find an automotive glass service willing to do the cutting. Top chopping on standard production cars is not unknown in most areas, and generally a hot rod supply can recommend someone who cuts curved glass.

A trick from the customizing shops for windshields works well on closed cars when the height needs to be less. The cowl area where the windshield would normally rest is sunk into the body, on a line with the windshield posts. This allows the windshield wipers to mount below the hood line, so that when the hood is extended back to the windshield the result is hidden wipers. Most new production cars are built this way, with a single-piece hood, and builders of sports-style closed cars find this method useful. It has been used successfully on a couple of open cars, as well.

Making windshield posts for a closed car is not too difficult, making windshield supports for an open car can be tedious. These supports

can be welded of metal, the production car posts can be heavily modified, or metal supports can be cast from bronze or machined from aluminum. Fiberglass supports for an open car are not entirely successful, although some contemporary street rod bodies use short stubs at either side of the windshield and a slot in the cowl for glass alignment. A novel and very satisfactory windshield solution for open sports car-style bodies is the use of a windshield from an older production sports car, such as the MG. The determining factor is width.

While it is possible to make windshields of a clear Plexiglas, such as Lexan, the results are never satisfactory. The plastic scratches easily, and state vehicle laws specifically state that safety glass is required for all windscreens.

Curved side glass is extremely difficult to work with. Contemporary curved side glass is tempered, making it nearly impossible to cut. The only satisfactory way to modify it is to have the glass normalized with heat, the cuts made, and then have the glass re-tempered. Very expensive. If curved glass is an absolute requirement for windows, the most successful homebuilders find something on a production car that will work and create the body design around the glass. Again, Plexiglas side windows work, but they do not prove totally practical.

Windshield posts on open cars must be supported in the body, this is usually done with metal plates under the cowl. The posts of a closed car can easily be overlooked as a weak point, metal or wood substructure in the glass area is highly recommended.

Most modern fiberglass car builders resort to glue-in windshields and back windows. While urethane is the common adhesive, recent research shows that urethane breaks down after years of exposure to ultraviolet rays. The cure is to shield the urethane with paint or plastic trim, or to substitute RTV commercial silicone. This comes in a black color, and it sets extremely fast (about three minutes). If you plan to use silicone, also plan on having help installing the glass. A nice windshield trim comes from a production car, such as a Chevrolet Blazer, fitting in the gap between glass and body.

A side window mechanism from a production car works fine in a homebuilt fiberglass car, as long as all supports and attachment points are securely fastened to the fiberglass door or body.

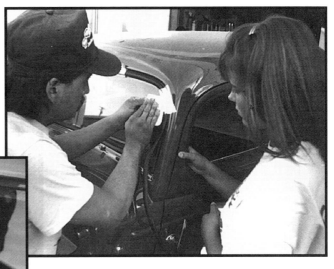

Hold the molding in place with masking tape, and make sure the molding is flush everywhere before adding a final sealant.

The opening behind the glass, which is the distance between the glass and the body flange, can be filled with either urethane or RTV commercial silicone (black). The silicone is less expensive and is supposed to last indefinitely. Between the urethane and the silicone there should be no water leaks.

TRIM

Trim is everything that is added to a body other than glass. Most of this bolts in place, some may be held by automotive-type trim clips, and at least part of the trim will be glued on. As a rule, only a small percentage of trim is cosmetic.

Head and taillights are trim, and they bolt in place. Back when the body mold was being designed, the location for these lights would have been determined. State vehicle laws dictate the legal height of these lights. Both headlights and taillights will use "buckets" to locate the light elements and the lens, these buckets should bolt to metal brackets that are laminated to the fiberglass.

A note about electrical wiring is in order. Because the body is fiberglass, it is necessary to run a grounding wire from every electrical component. This means lights, dash, everything electrical. The frame can serve as a common ground, for the sake of convenience.

Bumpers or hot rod-type Nerf bars may be part of the design. These must be attached via sturdy brackets directly to the frame. Do not bolt these to the body, since the body has little resistance to the type of shock a bumper must absorb. Small imported car bumpers work well on homebuilts, as do the new ribbed aluminum bumpers available through custom car and street rod magazine vendors.

Grilles have traditionally been transplanted from production cars, but it is often difficult to find a grille that really works with a special fiberglass body design. A grille can be cast from aluminum, but this requires a casting mold and finishing work. Many body builders make the grille from stainless steel sheet stock and round or square rod, in recent years it has become fashionable to mill a grille from a block of aluminum. The former is popular with craftsmen who can weld, the latter with machinists. A grille can also be made of fiberglass, over a special mold, but this takes almost as much time as casting something from brass or aluminum. If a sports-type body has been designed, the necessity for a grille is circumvented by creating a design that has a mouth, but no grille insert. An inexpensive grille can be made from expanded metal wire mesh, a variety that is available through most metal supply outlets.

Often the dash is not molded as a part of the body, but is laminated to the body later, or simply bolted to body brackets. Whether the body is open or closed, the dash can add considerable strength to the body in the cowl area. This is vital in an open-body style, where cowl shake can be a nuisance. If the dash is made of fiberglass, it should have a metal or wood reinforcement along its lower edge, from side to side. This reinforcement bolts or is laminated to the body, usually about four to six inches down on either front door post. If the dash is removable, the reinforcement should be part of the body structure. This dash reinforcement becomes the mounting support for the steering column.

Upholstery is a key element to making a fiberglass car both comfortable and good looking. But what is below the upholstery is vital! Fiberglass bodies do a fair job of deadening road sounds, but are poor insulators of temperature. It is possible to use some of the traditional woven materials for insulation, but far superior are the new foil sandwich insulators. These are advertised in the street rod and kit car magazines, but they are also available at most home building supply chain stores. Glue this sandwich material directly to the fiberglass panels and the floor, then add the upholstery.

While upholstery is not the theme of this book, it should be noted that many fiberglass closed-car builders have a problem with the windshield / window garnish molding. These were common to production cars well into the 1950s, but are no longer common. Fiberglass garnish moldings are thicker than the sheetmetal stampings, so they sometimes do not look really good. Enterprising builders have started having the closed cars upholstered without garnish moldings, drawing on modern car interiors for ideas, gluing the upholstery material in place directly to the fiberglass body. The result is excellent, a good upholsterer familiar with custom automotive work will know how this is done.

REPAIRS AND MODIFICATIONS

FIXING WHAT'S BROKE OR MAKING CUSTOM CHANGES

Making repairs to a new fiberglass body or part may seem a premature subject, but knowing how to repair fiberglass at the outset saves lots of headaches later. The same with making custom changes to the finished product, modifications that are sometimes easier made to the finished body than to the original mold (or come as an afterthought). The repairs or custom work referred to here is relative to a fiberglass body, not a metal body. This work will be done with polyester and / or epoxy resins, fiberglass cloth and matte, special urethanes such as RSP, and filler putties.

Do this work in a clean area, with low humidity, out of direct sunlight, and at a room temperature of about 75 degrees. Anything over 90 degrees makes the work very difficult due to extremely short resin kicking times, on the cold end use heat lamps to raise the work surface temperature.

Small scratches in the fiberglass gel coat sometimes can be polished out, larger gouges require filling with a putty. Polyester putty can be used but it will shrink), epoxy works much better. The area must be thoroughly cleaned, if acetone is used make sure it does not attack a painted finish. Gouge edges must be sanded, then catalyzed putty is applied with a pressing,

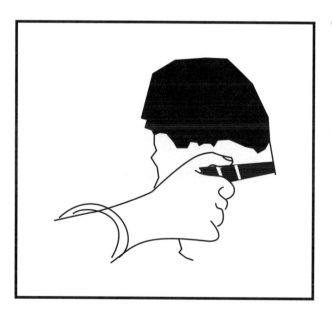

Use a power sander to feather edge the area around backside of the hole (or crack). If there is any underseal on the panel backside, this must be thoroughly cleaned away before sanding. Usually sand an area two to six inches from the edge of the opening.

If a fiberglass panel area is cracked, it is sometimes best to cut the entire area away so that a patch will connect with full-strength material. Use discretion on the size of hole, however.

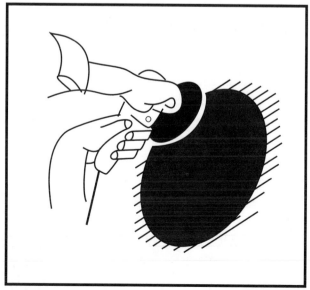

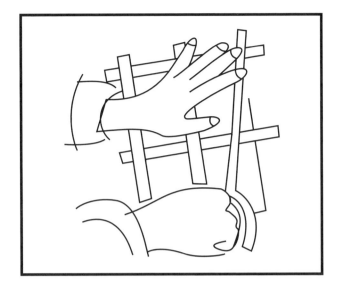

Make a backing on the front side of the panel, this can be of cardboard. Place cellophane between the cardboard and the fiberglass panel, and tape the backing firmly in place. A flexible piece of polypropylene sheet works just as well.

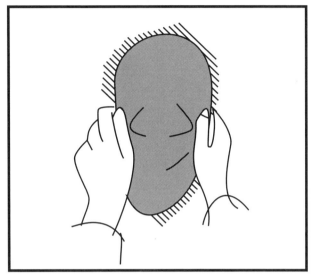

Cut two pieces of matte to the hole shape. Mix resin with hardener and brush on the inner surface (working from backside of panel) of the backup. Apply a piece of matte, saturate it with resin, then apply a second piece of matte.

wiping motion. Wipe the putty knife across the repair immediately to remove excess putty. After the putty has cured, sand with 100-grit followed by 240-grit sandpaper. Prime and finish with color. Follow this same procedure when repairing small cracks and crazing. Each hairline crack must be opened up by grooving, then repaired. Small holes may require more than putty, if so apply polyester or epoxy resin to the sanded area, then small patches of fiberglass matte are saturated, pressed into place, and allowed to cure. Use a general-purpose resin, so that the repair cures tack free. If more build-up is needed, sand the patch, and add more lightweight matte. Once the repair is higher than the surrounding laminate, rough it to shape with 80- to 100-grit sandpaper, and finish with 220-grit sandpaper. Finish with gel coat or paint.

Quite often, the homebuilder ends up with some extra holes in the body or fenders, holes that weren't intended or turn out not to be needed. Obviously, these are more than nicks, and they go through the laminate. It is common to fill these holes with putty, but this is a repair that isn't as strong as it could be. Some fiberglass laminated to the back of such a hole gives a foundation for the putty, but this is still not the best repair. It's best is to sand and bevel both sides of the hole. Sand out from the hole's edge half an inch or more (depending

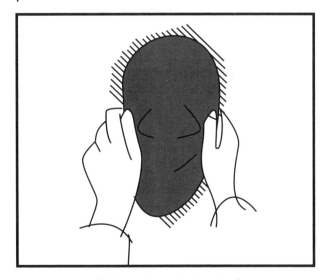

Cut pieces of fiberglass cloth, the first to overlap the hole edges by an inch, each successive piece of cloth will have a slightly larger overlap. With the resin in place, use a roller or squeegee to work out all air bubbles.

A crack in fiberglass is not difficult to repair, unlike metal the glass does not distort.

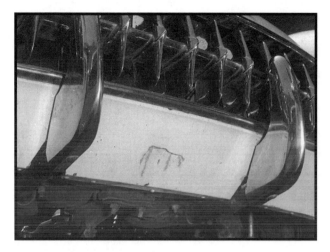

on the hole size). Make a back-up of cardboard or masking tape. If this is to be used on the smooth side, a piece of cellophane will keep the repair very smooth, this cellophane is directly against the smooth surface, supported by the cardboard or masking tape. Mix a batch of polyester or epoxy resin, coat the sanded area, and apply a matte patch just a tiny bit larger in diameter than the offending hole. Let this cure, sand the area, and apply more matte or cloth if needed. This isn't a major fill, so finish off with putty once the initial matte is cured.

If the gel coat is to be repaired, spray or brush on a very thin coat. When this cures, water sand with 400- and 600-grit sandpaper, then polish. Be gentle, the gel coat is very thin. If the gel coat is air-inhibited, cover it with a piece of cellophane, and tape the cellophane edges. This keeps out the air so the gel coat kicks tack free. The same result comes from spraying or brushing on a coat of polyvinyl

alcohol (PVA) as a sealer.

Although fiberglass is strong, it has a tendency to rupture under heavy impact. It will also crack under high stress, and even prolonged exposure to sunlight will cause it to deteriorate. Thus, you may need to repair damage sustained through a wreck, years of use, or rough treatment taking the part from a mold. It can happen at any time.

Impact damage is the most common, and it ranges from a small crack to an entire panel (or body). This kind of collision damage often shatters the fiberglass, and everywhere there is

This is the backside of that crack, the grille has been removed for convenience and the inside of the fiberglass has been ground with a power sander. In so doing, an area of fiberglass has been removed, leaving a hole.

Resin is mixed with hardener and brushed on the sanded area. Under normal conditions, polyester resin has a working time of about 30 minutes, this can be altered by the amount of catalyst or the temperature. Some repair epoxies are faster, some slower, same with some urethanes.

Fiberglass cloth is cut and set in place on fresh resin. This 'glass patch is saturated with more resin, then a second layer of 'glass is installed. Matte can also be used, but cloth is strongest.

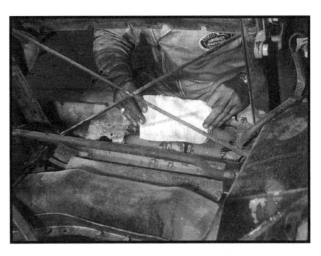

a crack or tear, the laminate has become delaminated! Seriously, look at the edges of the crack and note that the resin has shattered, leaving shredded fiberglass. Unlike metal, which deforms badly on impact, fiberglass simply breaks apart. Putting it back together is more a matter of patience and aligning the broken parts than of "straightening" anything.

If the damage is localized, a maximum of about two by two feet, you may have to patch a broken hole or just bad cracks. Either way, trim the broken glass away using a saw. The new "hole" thus created should have a rounded circumference, with no pointed edge anywhere. The idea is to trim away all the shattered and badly broken fiberglass, leaving a trimmed edge that is unfractured. Sand the inside of the body well back from the trimmed edge,

Lower section of front fender has been broken away, the area is sanded on the backside and the panel is put back in place. It can be held in place by a bar on the outside...

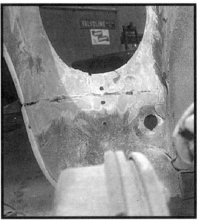

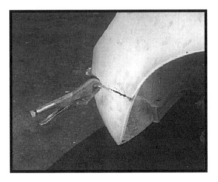

...or with a clamp. The idea is to get the pieces aligned perfectly before adding any repair fiberglass.

this distance is in direct proportion to the size of the hole to be repaired. Then bevel the inner and outer edges of the hole.

If at all possible, work from the inside of the panel first. Make a cardboard backing, and place cellophane between the panel and the cardboard. (The cellophane isn't essential, it

The repair seam is covered with a coat of resin, then fiberglass cloth or matte strips are laminated to back side. Overlap each strip to get maximum strength. Usually two or three layers of fiberglass are required on the inner side. On the outside, groove a tight-fitting join line for more surface area, then fill the groove with fiberglass strands mixed with resin. Sand this mix and finish with plastic filler.

A small hole in the fender lip is typical of imperfections that need attention, either on a crash repair or on a newly molded piece.

just makes the resin surface smoother.) Tape this backing to the panel, it will curve in one direction only.

Purchase a resin that has a higher viscosity than the resin you used to make the body. Most auto parts stores and marine supply outlets feature repair kits. Select a resin that is thick

enough for vertical and overhead work. This resin will be more difficult to saturate the fiberglass with, but not a major problem. Put a coat of resin on the backside of the panel, over the backup and the sanded area. Cut a piece of matte the size of the hole and set in place. On a large diameter hole, use strips of matte about three inches wide in succession until the hole is covered. Saturate the matte with the thick resin. It may be necessary to daub the wet matte several times to keep it in place until the resin starts to kick. A piece of dry fiberglass cloth may be held in place to retain the wet matte, then when the resin kicks the dry cloth can be saturated. The problem is simply keeping the matte in place until the resin hardens. Cut a piece of matte slightly larger, put this in place with more resin, repeat again as the matte is spread over a larger and larger area. It's not necessary, but makes a nice finish to use a piece of cloth as the final backside addition. Mix just enough resin and catalyst to do the job, this works out to about one pint of mixed resin to one square foot of fiberglass (makes two coats). This prevents loss of extra resin due to short pot life.

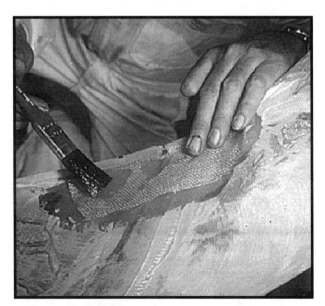

The inner surface is sanded, and a resin and fiberglass patch applied.

A headlight tunnel in an early Corvette is positioned, then an electric drill with a rotary file is used to roughen the areas where fiberglass will be used.

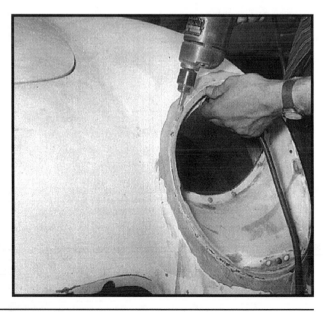

Remove the cardboard backup on the outside, and build up the patch with matte, overlapping the edges. The patch will be thicker than the original laminate, but the outer side will be worked down to match the panel contours. Use a power sander, starting with 36-grit paper and work the outside surface nearly level with the original panel. Use progressively finer sanding discs (up to 100 grit), then switch to a sanding board for final shaping. Finally, use a filler putty to get a perfect repair that is ready for primer.

An alternative for fixing a large hole is to make a match panel. Tape a piece of thin cardboard or posterboard to the damaged panel's outer surface. This should be larger than the hole by an inch or so. Lay small strips of saturated matte over the cardboard, building until the fiberglass is same size as the cardboard. Once this hardens, it can be placed behind the hole and laminated in place, with

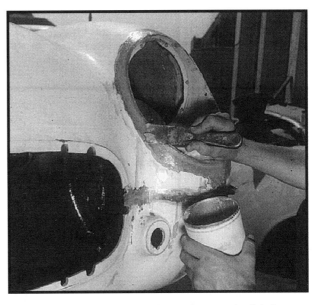

Strips of fiberglass cloth and resin hold the headlight tunnel to the fender, a vinyl ester filler putty can be used as an adhesive.

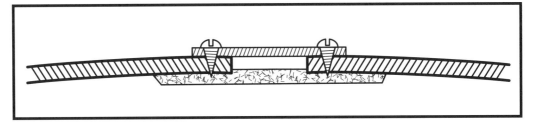

Broken pieces of fiberglass can be aligned and held in position by adding a bar on one surface, screws hold these bars in place. A fiberglass patch is added to the opposite side.

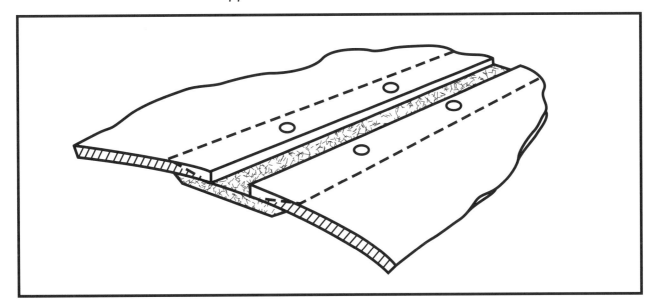

After the new patch has hardened, the alignment bars can be removed. The area from edges of break, back toward the good fiberglass, will be ground away to form a shallow trench.

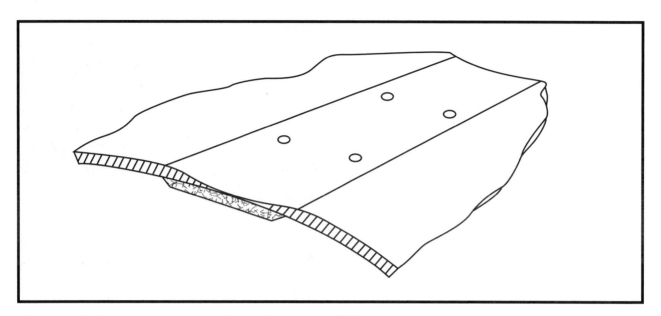

This trench does not need to be large, but it should be big enough to contain a substantial patch on the outer surface.

additional matte added on the outer side.

Another alternative is to tape some hardware wire to the back side of the hole, which has a small quarter-inch or so weave. It can be shaped to the panel contour before being taped in place. Saturate some matte and lay it directly on this mesh, working from the panel outside. You don't have to overlap onto the surface, just touch the damaged area edge

enough to temporarily hold the patch in place. Once the patch hardens, remove the wire mesh (vital), then cover the back side with more laminates of 'glass, lapping over the edge of the original panel. Once this support has hardened, finish the front side. Working with this mesh is one of the better ideas to come along, and it can become an excellent temporary mold base. Some fiberglass mesh tapes are on the

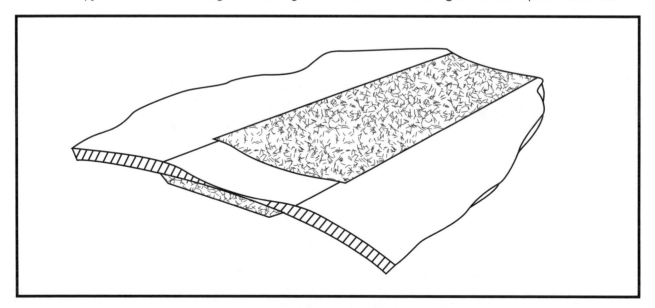

Fill the trench with matte, usually several layers are needed. The patched area will be thicker than the original fiberglass, for best strength, the outer surface will be finished with plastic filler. All air bubbles will be repaired, and a gel coat can be added prior to paint.

Custom fiberglass pieces can be molded and added to a fiberglass body easily. This Corvette fender flair has been attached with 'glass and resin, then plastic filler was used to make the surface perfect for paint.

market that will do the same job and are worth looking into.

If a very large area has been shattered, such as a fender that has been literally broken in two, your first job is to align the pieces. Block the largest loose section in place, then work with the smaller broken pieces to get everything back in position. It will probably be necessary to bridge over large broken areas with some kind of bar, this can be a metal strap, a length of wood, or whatever. This can be bolted or screwed to the fiberglass to hold everything in alignment, use as many of these bars as necessary. Clamps work for alignment, also. Vise Grips with deep throats are especially useful for clamping pieces together.

Once the major undamaged parts are back in position (measure and eyeball everything several times as a continuing check for fit), align the smaller broken sections with masking tape. The bars can be on either side of the panel, whichever is most convenient, remember to remove any screws or bolts once the parts are laminated back together. The smaller pieces become filler, helping bridge all the gaps as new fiberglass is laid on. Remember that both sides of each small piece need to be sanded to get new resin to bond.

Sand back from the damaged edges on both sides, then make a backup for the clear side of the panel (the side without the bars). Tape it in place and start adding fiberglass. Add strips

Fiberglass bodies can be modified in just about any way, the back portion of a 1923 Ford Model T body is here trimmed to fit on front portion of a 1927 Model T body.

It isn't necessary to get an exact fit between joining panels with fiberglass (unlike metal), since the gaps immediately fill with fiberglass and resin during any bonding.

It is essential that all surfaces of fiberglass that will get a new coat of resin and fiberglass are sanded thoroughly.

between the holding bars at first (avoid getting resin and 'glass on the bars), after these have cured, remove the bars and continue. A word of caution: The larger the patch, the harder it is to hold in place vertically or overhead. A patch about five by eight inches is the very maximum that can be worked at a time. Speeding the kick time of resin with more catalyst works up to a point, as does the addition of heat lamps. The real key to repairing large areas is patience, doing a small section at a time. Building up a lot of lost panel is tedious, but in some cases necessary. If you still have the body or part mold available, it is possible to make up a repair section. Trim the body and the repair section to get a butt joint, bevel the mating edges, sand well back from the edge on all pieces (both sides), and join. Repair sections for fiberglass production cars (such as Corvettes) are produced commercially and done this way.

A tack-free resin works nicely for patch work, since repeated sanding will be involved. As with any fiberglass work, always remove air bubbles during the laminating process, after the patch has cured, repair any air bubbles that show up. Do not use plastic filler instead of fiberglass and resin when making structural repairs or when bonding two pieces of panel. This is a filler, not a bonding agent.

In the event a repair is poorly done or panels are out of alignment, cut the sections apart and start again.

Customizing an area with fiberglass is straightforward. It is possible to make a male plug of foam or cardboard. This can be taped to the fiberglass body (adjacent areas on the body need to be sanded back from the joining line a couple of inches at least). A female mold can be made, but usually a single stage laminate is laid over the mold and laminated directly to the body. The rough outside of this

Small metal strips become holding bars to align the Model T body parts. A young Curt Hamilton, shown doing the work, was a pioneer in making hot rod bodies of 'glass.

laminate is sanded and finished with resin and / or plastic filler.

When making custom changes to a fiberglass body, it is best to add laminates of fiberglass, rather than throwing a bucket of plastic filler at the area. The fiberglass becomes a part of the body, thick filler may crack and fall away over time.

It is also popular to combine parts from two or more bodies. This works the same as adding a large repair section to an original panel. When combining panels, it is good practice to overlap successive patches by an inch or more each time, tapering each layer farther from the join line. This increases strength considerably.

Filler fiberglass may be of matte or resin impregnated fiberglass strands, this area is worked smooth and then regular plastic filler brings the connection seam up to par for finish paint.

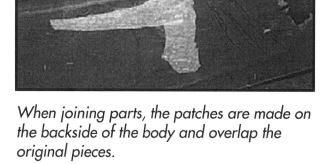

When joining parts, the patches are made on the backside of the body and overlap the original pieces.

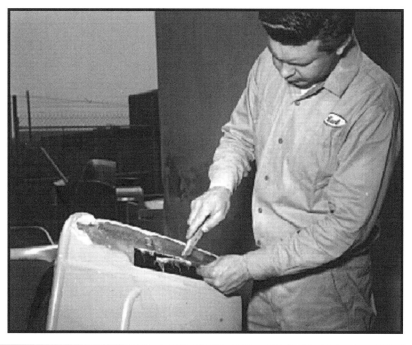

MAIL-ORDER BODIES & PARTS

READY-MADE FIBERGLASS CAR COMPONENTS FOR THE HOMEBUILDER

Up to now, this book has been devoted exclusively to creating your own fiberglass body or parts. You've done the designing, planning, and making of each component. It has been neither easy nor inexpensive. It has been a challenge, but in most respects doing something this demanding can be a pleasure. On the other hand, should you even go to the bother of making your own fiberglass car body? Given the cost and time involved, would it not be better to buy a commercial 'glass body and concentrate on assembling the chassis and body?

If you have a unique body design in mind, or a specialty part that is not available, you have no choice but build your own. This is definitely true of a full envelope sports-style body, or possibly a classic / antique replica. But if the body style is popular, chances are very good it is commercially available, at a price below what you can duplicate at home.

A larger, more diverse selection of manufactured fiberglass car bodies are available today than at any time. While a few special fiberglass "kit" cars were on the market starting in the early 1950s, it was the advent of hot rod Model T bodies in the late Fifties that started the industry. These bodies were meant for drag racing, initially, but were a natural for street roadsters. At the same time, some very radical sports car designs began appearing in the 1960s. These were mostly radical coupes, some for specially built chassis, and later, most were intended for the Volkswagen chassis.

It was the dune buggy fiberglass body that accelerated the kit car theme for fiberglass bodies. At first, these bodies required some VW chassis pan modifications, but soon the design was for an unmodified VW chassis. Manufacturers proliferated, to the point where the market was saturated. By the mid-

The fiberglass specialty car bodies have become so well constructed that many builders prefer 'glass to metal. Enthusiasts who want a quality product can assemble at home or have professionals do the job.

1970s, this phase of homebuilt specials had dwindled. Meantime, sports car bodies continued to evolve and hot rod bodies were taking on a level of sophistication once considered impossible. It was the hot rod area where fiberglass gained real acceptance as a serious body material. Early body styles in good or restorable steel came into very short supply, and fiberglass was the answer.

The original Model T fiberglass bodies gave way to Model A and 1932 Ford roadsters. Then came coupes and phaetons and sedans. Finally, phantom cars began to appear, body styles that were never created by a factory. Bodies that were exact replicas of an original came to the market, for hot rodding as well as a new area… pseudo classics.

Classic body styles were available with frames, ranging from the mighty Deusenburg touring to Cord. Some of these cars were available as turn-key drive-away versions, at hefty prices that tended to verify their credibility. Some were outstanding designs, others were marginal at best. At this time, a few manufacturers of questionable intent began to surface. Shoddy products teamed with shady business practices began to taint the image of the "kit car" industry. Hot rod manufacturers escaped the scandals, for the most part. There are still, unfortunately, a few disreputable suppliers of kit cars, so that potential sports car or classic car body buyers should make inquiries before sending money. Know exactly what you want, get every aspect of the transaction in writing (with exact delivery dates), and the exact amount of money involved. If possible, do a first hand inspection of a kit, and talk with the buyer. Interestingly, most of the problems associated with the marginal sources are with the chassis. By and large, fiberglass bodies are quite good.

Toward the end of the 1980s, fiberglass classic kit cars began to lose favor to more popular late-model styles, with the Cobra roadster the unquestioned leader. With this proliferation of later styles came more scrutiny from original manufacturers, who were concerned that the kit car quality would impact on their images. Soon, major makers such as Ford and Chevrolet stepped in to protect copyright names and logos, and in some cases to actually grant licenses.

Older hot rod body styles were never a concern to the factories. Although Ford continues to be the most duplicated body style, Chevrolet and Chrysler products are getting a share of the market. Body styles continue to diversify, with pickups and later model designs coming through manufacturing evolution. The 1949-52 Mercury body style opened new possibilities for the large late models, now 1955-57 Chevrolet bodies are available, and Mustang bodies are being developed.

The only way to get a current update on what is available is to scan periodicals that cater to enthusiasts. For hot rodding, a number of hot rod and street rod magazines carry ads for that style body. For sports cars, the best known publication is *Kit Car.* For antique / classic cars, ads run in *Hemmings Motor News, Old Cars Weekly,* and similar restoration-themed publications. Most ads offer catalogs, and it is often necessary to get the catalog to find out what an individual manufacturer offers. It may be a single body, often it is a full line of bodies and parts, some of which are not prominently featured. The larger suppliers of fiberglass bodies and parts also offer a full line of accessories. Shop the entire market for hard-to-find products and for the best prices.

Become aware of enthusiast events in your area. There are auctions, rod runs, car shows, nostalgia races, even specialty trade shows where these products are on display. This is an excellent opportunity to see the product first hand, to talk with the sales personnel, and to compare various manufacturing techniques.

Buying a ready-made fiberglass body, or individual parts, is a smart alternative to doing all your own fiberglass creation. Providing, of course, that someone makes what it is you are looking for. While the hot rod bodies go to both the homebuilder and the professional assembler, the sports and classic car bodies seem to tend toward the professional. These are often enthusiasts who have built several commercial-bodied kit cars, and who come into demand with people wanting such cars but having little time or inclination to do the assembly. There are some specialty car building firms that do nothing but this kind of assembly, in both the hot rod and sports or classic field. There have been instances, though, of shoddy or dishonest dealings from assemblers. Again, check the credentials of any prospective assembly person, often check on the progress in person, and have everything in writing.

On the following pages we have compiled a sampling of commercially available fiberglass products, from Model T Fords to Jeep styles. We walk you through some manufacturer's facilities, showing how the products are made, and we show you examples of cars being built. Soak up information from every page. It doesn't matter much whether you are building a chopped Mercury custom or a race car, a Jeep or a Cobra. The chassis may look different, but it is still just a wheeled platform onto which you bolt a fiberglass body.

In every case, however, it is vital to realize that none of this is a 30-minute exercise. It takes time to build your own fiberglass body. It takes time to bolt any body (yours or one from a manufacturer) onto a frame and make the entire vehicle complete. Patience becomes the necessary byword for any fiberglass car project.

IFG'S SLEEK SPORTS CAR

Although the Cobra-styled sports kit car is the reigning champion of popularity, it is still the replicas of very unusual sports cars that catch the eye of enthusiasts. Such a vehicle is the 25th Anniversary coupe (which looks to copy the Countach) from IFG, 15740 El Prado Rd., Chino, CA 91710. This very radical mid-engine car is based on the Pontiac Fiero chassis, which is an excellent platform for nearly any fiberglass car (your homebuilt body as well as a variety of commercial bodies).

The 5000S edition replica of the famous Countach is based on the 93.5-inch wheelbase Fiero chassis. The body is built with rain gutters and steel framework included, doors and other elements of this body can be pre-assembled as an option.

The Fiero front suspension can have larger front brakes as an options, neat thing about using a chassis such as this is the utilization of factory equipment for direct repairs or initial building.

If a small block GM type V8 engine is used, the Fiero chassis must be extended, seven inches were added to the chassis to accommodate this Corvette engine.

A Porsche transaxle assembly is mated to the Feiro suspension in this case. Most kit car manufacturers include all the necessary brackets for any options they may offer.

The IFG small block Chevy V8 engine kit includes crossmembers that bolt / weld in place, while the homebuilder can make brackets, in the long run it saves time to buy the ready-made items.

Chassis for IFG fiberglass bodies come in three basic lengths: Stock Fiero, extended 5 inches to 98.5 inches, and extended 7 inches for the small block Chevy engine. This extension is made just behind the cockpit.

This IFG open body sports car is on the 7-inch extended chassis with a small block Chevy engine. Most sports car body suppliers have a wide array of styles, prices will vary from moderate to high.

The 25th Anniversary edition is on the 5-inch extended chassis; it includes two side air scoops. The IFG series, as well as a number of other sports / classic car assemblies, can be ordered in several stages of pre-assembly.

OFF-ROAD JEEP STYLE

This particular vehicle was a project for an off-road magazine, built by well-known automotive journalist Richard Johnson. The assumption that created the project was that no single Jeep vehicle included all of the best elements of all the years the Jeep has been in production. Richard's solution was to plan a vehicle that included the best ideas, along with mechanical elements that are still available. Since this was to be a kind of dream car, a fiberglass body was selected. These bodies are used in competition, but they are designed to accept stock Jeep parts, so they work equally well for a daily driver.

The stock Jeep frame is a very straightforward ladder style, with two parallel boxed frame rails connected by simple crossmembers. The semi-elliptic springs at all corners can be lowered or raised depending on desired height of the vehicle, there is a huge selection of aftermarket performance equipment available for any off-road vehicle. Most pickup and off-road frames are very similar to this one, tread widths are similar but wheelbases will vary.

The fiberglass body is set on the chassis to get an idea of what work might be needed. Unless components are mixed, this is usually a simple bolt-on situation. The wheel well openings at the rear are aligned with the tires, the front panels can be set in place to make sure they fit the wheelbase. A body such as this can be modified to suit any use.

Since the fiberglass body was not going to have modifications or other fiberglass added to the floor underside, it was turned over and prepared for a paint undercoating. This is primarily a cosmetic treatment.

Any modifications or repairs needed on a commercial body can be done with the epoxy repair materials available through most auto and marine supply stores. This body is from 4WD Hardware, Inc, 44488 State Route 14, Columbiana, OH 44408.

Fiberglass is not as heavy as metal, but it isn't balloon-weight, either. After the firewall and floor underside has been painted and undercoated, it is set in place. The chassis should have all modifications and repairs made, then the paint is added, prior to installing the body.

After the body was checked for fit, it was removed and the chassis set up with a full roll cage. This is more important with a fiberglass body than with one of metal. The engine for this project was a new 4.3 liter Chevy V6. Eventual performance was very impressive.

Large metal plates for body bracing were welded to the frame, via tubing supports. This spreads the twisting and shock forces over a large area to prevent body fractures.

Front panels for the Jeep-style body allow you to use nearly any radiator, an important consideration if a larger engine is selected. The radiator should fit in a metal mount off the frame, not be bolted precariously to the fiberglass panels.

The better commercial fiberglass bodies are built to accept readily available accessories, such as this fabric top.

Any small brackets need to be supported on the backside of the fiberglass with large washers or metal plate. The fiberglass will soon fracture around bolt holes otherwise.

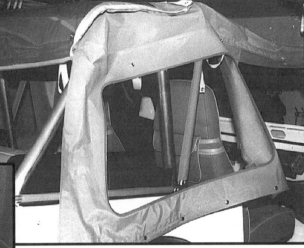

Although snap ferrules will usually stay in place without a backup to the screw, it is best to add small metal tabs inside the body as insurance against rough usage.

Accessory windshield wiper assemblies are available through street rod and off-road suppliers, and several good versions can be scrounged from junkyard cars. The slots above an electric wiper motor are for defroster air, a little item not to be overlooked in designing the fiberglass car dash area.

Virtually every fiberglass car, with a homebuilt or a commercial body, will need a steering column and custom steering wheel. Special columns are available through street rod suppliers, and wheels are everywhere. This custom dash is a piece of rectangular aluminum covered with engine-turn swirls.

Bumpers can never be bolted to a fiberglass body, everything must attach directly to the frame. This Warn winch is a handy addition at the rear of the Jeep.

Nearing completion, the vehicle (called the Ultimate Jeep in magazine articles) assembly time is numbered in weeks.

Another Warn winch up front, headlights in place, and it finishes the project. Building a fiberglass off-roader is not quite as complicated as a sports car or hot rod, but still requires lots of patience.

Fiberglass needs protection from the sun or it will deteriorate over time. The new two-part paints work especially well on fiberglass.

1927 Model T Roadster

Building a special car was once a process of scouring wrecking yards and scrounging used parts, from suspension components to body panels. Not so anymore. The aftermarket industry for hot rods, customs, and sports specials has grown to the point where it is possible to buy every component as a newly manufactured item. This has made the construction of fiberglass-bodied homebuilts very attractive, either by an individual who does his own work or by a professional who assembles the cars for others.

Although this type of assembled car is slightly restrictive in design, due to the types of components available, the results can be very attractive. This particular car was created by Brian Brennan as an exercise to show what could be purchased for such a car through the most unlikely mail-order source of Sears. The fiberglass 1927 Model T body is from Ai (Anderson Industries), the frame is from the Deuce Factory, but enough other items were available through the Sears automotive catalog to encourage the most novice of builders to give it a try. Assembly was by Darrel Zip and Magoo's street rod shop.

The 1926-27 Ford Model T body style is a good one for a hot rod, and it takes just a bit of part mixing to create a significant difference in designs. This body affords limited passenger room, roughly comparable to an imported sports car of the pre-Sixties.

Many of the fiberglass body and parts suppliers also have specialty frames and suspension components available, making it a one-stop shopping commitment for the buyer. Generally speaking, hot rod body styles are any styles dating from 1948 and earlier, customs are 1949 and later, and sports cars can be any year. However, the sports type fiberglass car is almost always referred to as a kit car, even though the hot rods and customs are in reality kit cars.

The fiberglass T body sits atop a new replica 1932 Ford frame. Every part of the suspension and power train for this car is brand new. The most serious piece of shop equipment for such a venture is an electric welder, a heavier duty MIG welder does nicely, and even this part of the assembly can be farmed out to a local welding specialist.

The floor for the T body is plywood. The back panel is also of plywood and can have a large area cut in the panel as a swing-away access to the trunk area (in case a working deck lid is not wanted). This panel can be installed after the body is bolted to the frame, diagonal measurements of the area ensure that the body is "square."

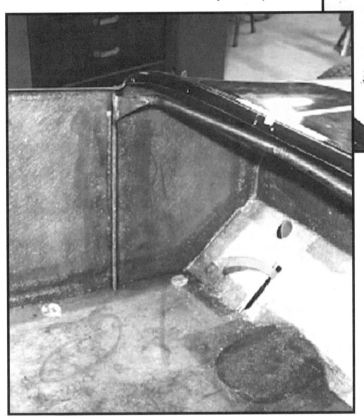

With the engine installed in the frame, the footboard can be cut from plywood and 'glassed between the firewall and the floor. A small transmission hump was needed, this can be molded in fiberglass over any kind of a temporary mold. An access slot for the brake pedal can be cut with a saber saw with the body in place. Take some extra time to determine exactly where the steering shaft will pass through firewall. Patching either fiberglass or wood to cure a mistake is easily done.

The firewall is cut away to clear the transmission during the body fitting stage. The steering shaft hole in the firewall is mostly an eyeballed measurement. Note how the hood / radiator support tubing has a larger flange where it attaches to firewall. This spreads the loads, it is best to have a metal strap on the inside of fiberglass as well.

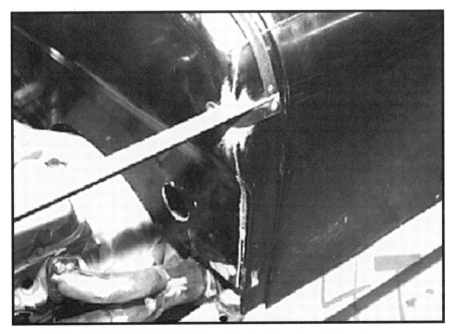

Special radiators are available for a wide range of cars, making it easy to select one for any kind of fiberglass body.

Grille shells and grille inserts are available for many different hot rod body styles, the selection is very limited for customs and almost non-existent for a home-created sports car. The popular kit cars usually include grilles and inserts. This chopped 1932 Ford grille shell is of fiberglass, and costs a fraction of what a metal swap meet item will cost.

Very few of the older modular-type hot rod bodies call for a fiberglass hood, simply because such a hood is easily bent from aluminum or sheet metal. A few sports car styles have these straight hoods, but no customs do.

This is a metal 1927 Model T body. The instant giveaway is the two opening doors, the cowl flap, and how the upholstery is done around rear of the cockpit.

Same body style, but this one is in fiberglass. Note that there is no cowl vent and how the upholstery of the seat fits body. A fiberglass 1932 grille shell and insert change the character of the style instantly.

This fiberglass T body has opening doors, but the seats fit into the body rather than roll over the back. The chopped windshield is complimented by a channeled body and cut down Model T grille shell. Trying to get the driver down behind the windshield in a car built so low becomes a major problem.

The C-Cab Delivery T offered a departure from more common roadster configurations. Several different fiberglass companies offered these bodies, and some are still available on special order.

Fad Ts often included many antique features, this one includes a brass radiator, rear view mirror, and top designs of a factory T.

This design is very typical of the 'glass-bodied '23 Ts of the 1960s era, with drag slicks and open exhaust headers. These cars incorporated many of the practical design elements of drag race cars.

THE FIBERGLASS FAD T

The most popular fiberglass body in hot rod history is the 1923 Ford Model T. This body has a very short cowl section that necks down at the hood, which restricts foot room drastically (as compared to the '27 and later Ford styles). The styling is definitely in the antique / classic car theme, which is part of its wide appeal to car enthusiasts and the general public alike.

These cars were nicknamed "Fad T's" during the 1960s, because there were so many of them on the street. Although they tend to be used for short trips, some hot rodders have put hundreds of thousands of miles in them on cross-country jaunts. There has been an interesting evolution of this hot rod body style. Originally the shortened Ts were called modifieds, in reference to their classification for racing at the Southern California dry lakes. During the 1960s, some rather garish designs began to appear at car shows, then during the 1970s the emergence of street rod runs dictated a more practical, road-worthy design. These fiberglass-bodied Model Ts continue to be the least expensive hot rods to create, if the design is one of moderation.

The evolution of early Model T modifieds is evident in this trio displayed at a recent Los Angeles Roadster Club show. The nearest car is an example of Fad T styling, while the two roadsters at the right run sans top and are built lower to the ground (more in keeping with early dry lakes modified styling).

Although there have been many manufacturers of fiberglass T bodies, most of the bodies include the shortened pick-up bed rather than a turtle deck. Chassis are readily available from many sources, and types of suspension vary widely.

Note the coil / shock horizontal suspension incorporated with a dropped tube axle. The rear-end of this car is a popular Jaguar independent.

Most Fad Ts run a full- or nearly full-height windshield, which is necessary because the occupants sit high in the body. The large windscreens often need support rods between the windshield and the chassis because of wind deflection on the glass. This can be a critical problem on open fiberglass car bodies.

As the Fad Ts evolved into the 1980s and 1990s, the trend has been getting the frame and body lower to ground and reducing windscreen height. An exaggerated rear tire size continues to be popular, but many of the chassis improvements typical of other hot rods and sports cars are in wide use.

Part of the contemporary Fad T styling is a retention of classic era items. Here the folding windshield and brass radiator add considerable charm.

Because the fiberglass T body is easily modified, many builders prefer to make changes. Here the seat back has been raised to increase seat height and comfort. Note the one-piece windshield.

Most fiberglass-bodied Ts are very lightweight, only a few run fenders. The supercharger tends to accentuate the appearance of horsepower, but the illusion is usually backed by tremendous acceleration.

1929 Model A Roadster

Brian Brennan decided a Model A roadster project would suit his magazine readership just fine, but this time the project would include a combination of salvage parts and a new fiberglass body from Ai. To keep everything running smoothly and on schedule, Brian asked Dick Magugorac (of Magoo's) to supervise the construction and assembly. Again, this is a construction process that anyone can do at home, with a moderate number of tools and a maximum amount of patience. Fortunately, magazines such as *Hot Rod Mechanix* include enough how-to articles in each issue for any novice to be successful. Our own book series includes *How To Build Real Hot Rods, How To Build Custom Cars, Specialty Car Electrical Systems,* and other titles that offer in-depth instruction on building a complete car. In this section, we are hitting only the highlights of fiberglass body usage.

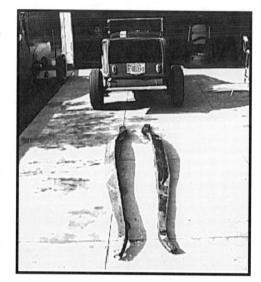

The frame side rails are from an original 1932 Ford frame. These are preferred over the straight Model A frame rails as they automatically lower the car several inches. New crossmembers will be fabricated, but lots of work will go into making the original rails nearly perfect.

This is a traditional hot rod, it is a contemporary hot rod, and it is a semi-kit car (in that not all the pieces were bought from aftermarket sources). By doing most of the work at home, a builder can expect to create such a roadster for under $20,000, sometimes way under. Fiberglass bodies eliminate much of the work on a typical homebuilt.

The frame rails must be sandblasted to eliminate all rust. After repair the rails are primed with a good sealer.

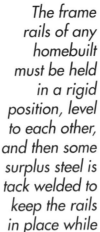

The frame rails of any homebuilt must be held in a rigid position, level to each other, and then some surplus steel is tack welded to keep the rails in place while crossmembers are added. Measurements for this chassis are available. A special body / chassis will need lots of planning before actual welding.

Once the rails are temporarily located, bar clamps keep them in place while working out the frame centerline with a string between center of the front and rear crossmembers. The rails can be moved until alignment is obtained, more temporary bars are then tack welded in place.

Before any final welding to the frame, the body is set in place several times to make sure the alignment is maintained as crossmembers are added.

On the 1929 Model A body, the frame was set slightly narrower at the firewall than a stock 1932 measurement, easy to do while setting up new crossmembers.

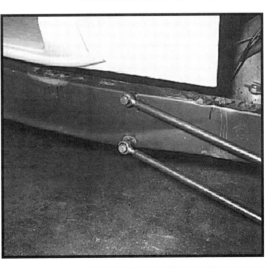

As the suspension is added, any modifications to the frame should include an additional fitting of the body during the process. Here rear location of the four-bar front suspension is added to the frame.

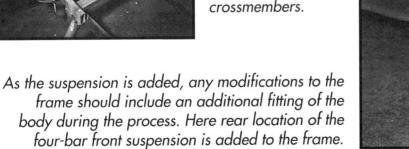

The engine and transmission are positioned relative to the body firewall and the radiator location over the front crossmember. The center crossmember is made up and welded to the frame. Note that where the crossmember attaches to the frame a short section of the frame rail has been boxed. The entire length of the frame rail can be boxed if desired to gain more torsional rigidity.

The dropped tube axle and spindle combination is bolted to the front spring, then shock absorber brackets are put in place temporarily.

The shock bracket is welded to the end of the frame rails. All of the finish welding and grinding is done only after the entire chassis is stripped bare.

The frame and suspension components can be painted once everything is welded and ground clean. During final assembly, pay particular attention to lock washers and / or cotter pins on all suspension components.

Run all brake lines so no abrasion can result, take extra pains to get hydraulic lines correct.

The steering box's location on the frame depends on the builder preference. Getting the shaft between box and steering column at the firewall is a just matter of cut and try.

With the engine in place, the body is set in alignment and the area for the transmission hump is marked on the plywood floor. This is cut for clearance, and the body is bolted to the frame with some kind of insulators between the floor and the frame.

The types of taillights used dictate where they fit on the body. License plate location can be determined early on and marked on the body for reference. All electrical items on the fiberglass car must have individual ground wires to the frame.

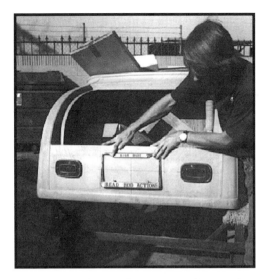

Most fiberglass cars come without the dash installed, and there are several different dash designs available. This body is using a recessed Auburn style dash, which is held in place while attachment is contemplated. The dash can be fiberglassed to the body or bolted in place.

All specialty fiberglass cars probably need aftermarket instruments. The location of the gauges is determined by working from a horizontal and vertical centerline marked on the dash.

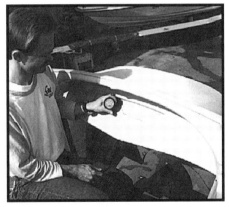

Purchase the gauges before cutting the dash! The number and size of the gauge head determines the gauge layout.

Mark out the gauge holes in the dash and drill a centering hole in the fiberglass. If you make a mistake, repair with fiberglass and start again.

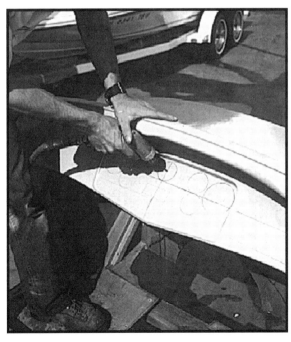

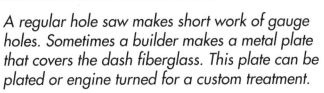

A regular hole saw makes short work of gauge holes. Sometimes a builder makes a metal plate that covers the dash fiberglass. This plate can be plated or engine turned for a custom treatment.

Other elements for the dash should be carefully located and fitted, taking into account clearance problems behind the dash.

Once the firewall hole for the steering has been cut, any mistakes can be cured with fiberglass. This hole is almost never done right the first time.

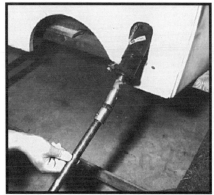

It is important to use only premium-quality universal joints in the steering system, good ones are advertised in most of the hot rod magazines.

On nearly every fiberglass car, the dash is not strong enough to support the steering column. A metal tube is run from the dash lip to the firewall and bolted in place.

The type of steering column selected is a personal choice. This one is a collapsible unit from a late model GM product. Brackets welded to the shaft housing hold the column to the dash and to the firewall.

The steering column is held in place temporarily to determine where the upper mounts should be (the clearance between the steering wheel and the driver's body as well as the left door are important considerations), and where the column should pass through the firewall.

Once the steering column location has been determined, the mounting plate is bolted to the firewall. Moving the steering column only a slight amount may be all that is needed to get steering shaft clearance at the engine.

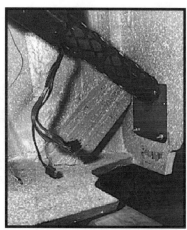

The inside surfaces of all fiberglass cars are usually very rough, it helps to clean up the appearance by spraying with a spackled-type paint finish. Paint everything in sight.

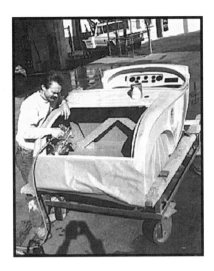

Spray even the trunk and under the dash. This doesn't stop the fiberglass from having an odor as it cures, but it helps the appearance.

Bolt the body to the chassis, add the details (such as upholstery and folding top), and you're on the road. But, expect some unexpecteds. Brian Brennan pauses on trip from Los Angeles to the Midwest to note a leaking gas tank.

1931 FORD PHAETON

It was the advent of the larger hot rod fiberglass bodies that elevated composite construction to the status of "real hot rods." Although Wescott was building Model A coupe bodies and fenders in the late 1950s, it wasn't until the 1932 Roadster started hitting the marketplace in the late Sixties that the "bigger" rod bodies became widely used. Even then, it was the introduction of brand new frames and chassis components that set the popularity wave in motion.

Finding a logical gas tank location for the Model T and Model A bodies can be a problem since the original tank was in the cowl. In 1932 Ford moved the tank to frame horns at the back of the body, when using the A frame, a neat solution is to add frame horns. Since a late model rear end is used in this installation, mounts for special coil-over shocks are welded to outer ends of the A crossmember.

It is often necessary to make clearance cuts in a fiberglass body, in this case the area over the crossmember center hump needed modification.

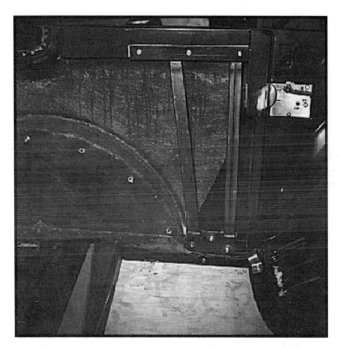

The Gibbon body uses steel tubing supports in the door post area to increase strength. Fiberglass bodies use an assortment of door latches, from new production original design to the modern bear claw.

In an effort to get the body / frame as low as possible, a "C" is cut in the frame directly over the rear end housing. This allows enough suspension travel to make the car road worthy.

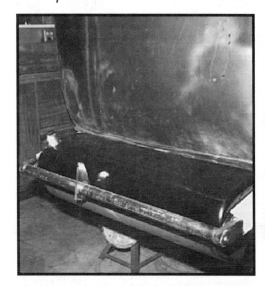

An aftermarket stainless steel gas tank is bolted to the newly installed frame horns, then a fiberglass 1932 gas tank cover is installed.

In the case of this body, the Model A frame cover apron is metal, which makes fitting the body to the frame easier. The firewall is pop riveted to the body, it can be 'glassed into one piece at a later date.

It usually takes some tweaking of fenders and other fiberglass cover pieces to get everything lined up and bolted together. Once all the parts are together, the 'glass will take a set.

Wherever possible, stock brackets are used to hold the fiberglass parts in place.

A modified headlight bar may not be exactly the same as the original, so test fit everything before sending metal parts out for paint or chrome.

All fiberglass has some minor shrinkage, which is why everything must be pulled into place and clamped during assembly.

Every electrical component on a fiberglass-bodied car must be grounded. In this case the headlight bar connects directly to the metal fender brace, which bolts to the frame.

The stock Gibbon body was molded to use a 1930-31 windshield frame. Since a custom windshield post was to be used, the post area was cut open for access. Once the new post is installed, the fiberglass will be rebuilt to fit.

Windshield posts are available from aftermarket sources, or they can be made by the homebuilder.

In this case, the windshield post was designed to extend down into a metal tube that bolts to the door post and the frame. With the frame level and the body bolted in place, the posts were aligned so that the windshield would not be in a bind.

In place, the new windshield post is a one-piece unit. If the post were to bolt to the body surface, a metal plate would be necessary under the cowl since the fiberglass is not strong enough for support.

Original exposed door hinges are used for this application, special hidden hinges are an option with most fiberglass body manufacturers. The recessed fiberglass dash panel does not fit the Model A body perfectly. Masking tape in the corners can be trimmed to the correct shape, the dash removed and fiberglass added.

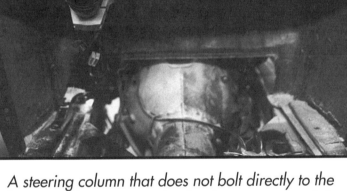

Steering column mounts vary widely, some sort of metal support is needed behind the dash.

A steering column that does not bolt directly to the frame will have too much vibration movement, it is imperative to have a good mount at the firewall.

Seating in any fiberglass car is a personal choice. Since this is a two door, the seat backs must fold forward for back seat access. Tapered wooden blocks make good mounts between the plywood floor and seat bases.

ZIPPER MOTORS

Zipper Motors is tucked away in the red cliffs of the Colorado National Monument in Durango, Colorado. Darrell Zipp has been associated with the specialty car business for most of his life. His background includes the Art Center College of Design. Later came work in industrial design, engineering, marketing and manufacturing, manager of research and development at Revell, and hands-on construction of street rods at Magoo's. Quite an impressive resume.

Back in the 1970's, Zipp formed the Traditional Street Rods company with Jim Skog and led the industry by manufacturing the first closed fiberglass 1932 three-window coupe. In 1986, Zipper Motors was created as a full-service street rod shop, able to take a project from concept design to turnkey completion. After building a number of one-off custom curved windshield roadsters, the idea was formulated to restyle a 1932 Ford roadster that could be manufactured with the curved windshield as part of the design. This would require a totally new fiberglass body. The Diamond Anniversary Deuce and Vikki Phaeton are the results.

In December of 1993, Zipp relocated from Southern California to Colorado, where Jim Skog rejoined the firm to handle all fiberglass work. Continuing the theme of a complete specialty car facility, the company creates everything needed for the homebuilder, as well as making drive-away cars. Check the source guide for contact information.

The Zipper roadster is a radical departure from traditional Ford Deuce construction, with front doors that are much wider, extending well into the cowl area so that there is a single opening line at the hood. The curved windshield is recessed into the body along the cowl top, stubby windshield supports are built into the cowl at either side. The optional fiberglass top is in the three-window coupe tradition.

A special hood of aluminum and hinged at the windshield line was created for the Zipper cars.

The phaeton is essentially the roadster from the door posts forward, with the larger second seat area added where the deck lid was. This becomes a phantom in the truest sense, a special fiberglass top is also available for the phaeton.

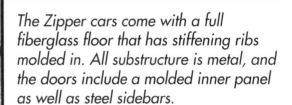

The Zipper cars come with a full fiberglass floor that has stiffening ribs molded in. All substructure is metal, and the doors include a molded inner panel as well as steel sidebars.

Once the steel substructure is in place, the phaeton body is very strong. A storage area is available behind the rear seat back. Lap and shoulder belt anchors are built into the steel framework.

The modern rear view mirrors blend well in the Zipper design, independent front suspension uses unequal length A-arms and coil-over shocks. The result of eliminating the original cowl lines is a sleek look not normally associated with the older Ford design. The windshield is laminated safety glass.

SPEEDWAY MOTORS

S peedway Motors of Lincoln, Nebraska, is a pioneer in fiberglass car bodies and parts, making products for street rods, kit cars, and circle track racers. Founded in 1952 by a young Bill Smith, the company began producing fiberglass in 1955, and was the first on the scene with a 1932 Austin and a 1927 Model T body.

All Speedway bodies are made as a unit, rather than in pieces that are assembled to make a body. Both metal and wood are used as substructure. Compound curves usually can be shaped easier in wood, and wood expands and contracts at a rate similar to fiberglass. When a threaded fastener is required, steel is usually used. Adhesives are used to bond reinforcements so as not to transfer or cause "print through" of the reinforcement to the outside surface of the panel. This print through is caused by thermal conductivity, and many times it can only be detected during the priming and painting process or after the painting and polishing have been completed.

Speedway bucks, or plugs, are made in a variety of ways and with a variety of materials, depending on what the product is. For example, to make a stock reproduction part, an original steel part may be used as the plug. A part that has been modified, or an original design, may be made from one or all of of the following: wood, fiberglass, body filler, cardboard, steel or foam. Molds and bucks are replaced as necessary to keep product quality at maximum levels.

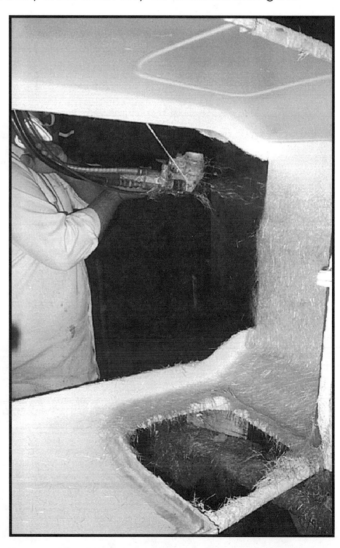

Polyester resin and fiberglass are used for all parts. Segments can be joined in or out of the mold, but they are joined in the mold when possible. Some products require customer work, others are delivered ready to use, such as pre-hung doors on the 1934 Ford pickup and the 1932 / 34 Ford roadsters. The roadster bodies are mounted to a frame when the doors are mounted to ensure they operate properly. Some reinforcements are added by the factory, some must be laminated by the customer, such as steering column or master cylinder supports.

Products may be a combination of lay-up processes, in some cases only the spray-up chopped strand method is used, in others a hand lay-up is required. This 1923 Model T mold is being filled with chopped strands. The single original right hand door is molded separately.

Female fender molds are made of fiberglass and mounted to sturdy supports for storage. A mold is replaced as needed.

Chopped fiberglass is sprayed on with special chopper guns, the result is a very strong panel with the right 'glass-to-resin ratio. Most Speedway products are cured in the mold for one day, larger bodies cure for about three days in the mold.

An array of fender molds sits in storage; each is marked for easy identity. Through the years Speedway has built up a considerable inventory of these bucks.

A pair of rear fenders and a complete 1923 Model T body await shipment. Most fiberglass bodies and large pieces travel via truck lines, the light weight keeps costs minimal.

Small pieces may require a hand layup, bonding adhesive is used when pieces must be joined.

TOTAL PERFORMANCE, INC.

Total Performance, out of Wallingford, Connecticut, is one of the nation's oldest producers of fiberglass-bodied hot rods. Available in kit and turnkey form, the Total cars have been available in a wide variety of body styles. Their most popular cars remain the 1923 Model T and the new 1927 Pro-Street roadster.

Total no longer laminates its own fiberglass, preferring to contract this work out and concentrate on quality control by working with local fiberglass constructors. Since turnkey cars are part of the line, the all-body design stresses ease of assembly. Molds are constructed with machining and drilling locations, with updates as necessary. All the bucks are built by Total, masters are constructed first for the Total line, then deviations added so the bodies will fit other products. All tooling is repaired and updated yearly to increase unit life, and never leaving a mold

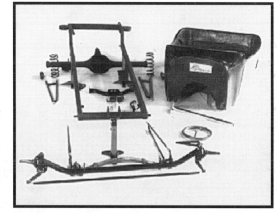

The basic Total T mail-order package may consist of virtually anything in this package, for the homebuilder the fiberglass body and the frame / front / rear suspension assembly is all that is needed for a rather rapid and low-cost assembly.

empty of a part has always protected molds not in use. Jigs and fixtures give consistency to the fiberglass.

All fiberglass is created by the chopper gun method, with minor addition. After the gel coat has set, all parts receive hand lay-up matte along the part periphery. This eliminates one potential for defects. After this step, the balance of the part is sprayed with the chopped fiberglass and rolled. New ultra-light biased ply fiberglass material is used. Originally discovered in the aircraft industry, this material is rather expensive, but it will not tear and it is vibration-proof. All bodies are oven cured for four hours at 300 degrees, to stabilize the product and eliminate the fiberglass smell. By utilizing fiberglass for structural strength, only a limited use of steel or wood is needed for the substructure. Wood is installed in the bodies for attaching interior panels.

The builder supplies the engine, normally, as well as the rear end gears and axles. Everything else that needs to be fabricated is part of the kit package.

Since little or no welding is needed to complete a kit of this type, the frame can usually be painted and final assembly started right away. First off is to get the chassis in a rolling state. Because they are far less complicated than the sports-style kit cars, the hot rod Ts are considered the most economical for entry-level street rodding.

Although nearly everything about assembling a kit car, rod custom or sports, can be done alone, it is nice to have some buddies handy. Here the frame is held in place while the rear coil-over suspension is bolted in place. Use lock washers, nylon lock nuts, or cotter keyed nuts everywhere on the suspension.

Total Performance owner Mickey Lauria is a practicing car enthusiast, he gets involved in nearly every phase of specialty car construction. Here he does the honors of lowering an engine into place.

An interesting thing about building a manufactured fiberglass car body is that most of the pieces needed to finish the body are part of the kit, which means much of the body can be assembled before the body is placed on the frame. Again, it's a nice time to include friends.

Positioning the body to the chassis is made easier when the floor-to-frame bolt holes are already drilled.

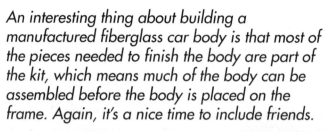

Once the body is in place, the wiring can be installed. It is highly recommended that one of the aftermarket vendor wiring harnesses be used, these are advertised in street rod and sports kit car magazines. With such a good kit, wiring takes just a few hours.

The Total T makes room for the battery under the seat, other electrical components are often placed under the seat as well. It is wise to cover all exposed "hot" wires with some kind of insulator to prevent unintended grounding and subsequent fire.

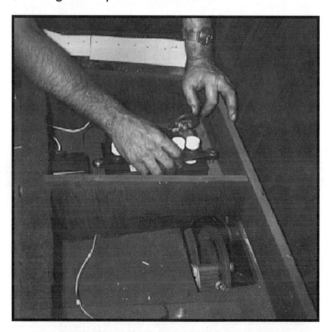

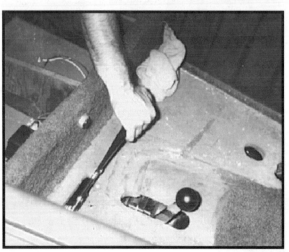

The hot rod body seldom has an abundance of room in the driving area, particularly the Model T. Here the shifter is placed to the transmission tunnel's right side, and the hand brake lever is mounted sideways just ahead of the seat.

HOW TO BUILD FIBERGLASS

All mounting brackets for the steering are included in the Total kit, dash gauges as well if desired. Remember to ground all electrical equipment.

Gas tank location is a problem in nearly every fiberglass car, the small pickup bed of a Model T is especially restrictive.

Interior kits are available for many kit rods; this is an effective way to minimize upholstery costs.

This Fad T style from Total includes the very early Model T fenders with upsweep, to change styles is mostly a matter of changing fenders and braces or running without fenders.

Once a car has been assembled, it is absolutely essential to make a check list of all the fluids needed. Go over the car very carefully to make sure all the bolts are secured and tight, set the front end geometry, and test run the engine prior to a slow and careful test drive.

This early style Total T is the kind that has come to be called a Fad T, but with only minor changes it can be a hot rod of any era.

The fenders and the tall top identify one styling trait, many owners of this kind of car keep the same vehicle for decades, only making changes to stay in touch with current trends.

1932 CHEVY THREE-WINDOW COUPE

As the variety of Ford-style fiberglass bodies continued to expand in the 1970s and 1980s, the demand for non-Ford styles grew, to the point where several manufacturers began to create such products. One of those suppliers was Class Glass & Performance of Cumberland, Maryland. The company has a 1932 Chevy roadster available, as well as the coupe, and some unusual additional pieces, such as 1939-47 Dodge pickup rear fenders, taillight recess tunnels for the Chevy bodies, etc. Following is a recap of building the coupe body, from beginning to end.

The Chevy coupe mold with separation flanges in place, is covered entirely with gel coat in preparation of laying on the fiberglass and resin. Most of the steps outlined here apply to any body being produced.

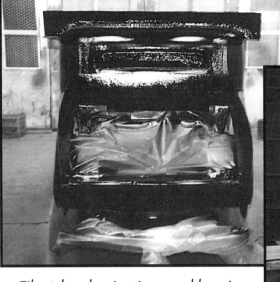

The first coats of gel are orange, followed by a coat of black as a back-up to show the gel coat thickness in the event a repair should have to be made in the mold itself.

Fiberglass laminations and bracing have been applied to the mold. The flanges where the mold must be separated have been drilled and bolted together, note the firewall flange has been trimmed in a curve on the left side.

Hollow half-round fiberglass tubes are molded to the buck to give extra mold rigidity, the original car for this mold was a steel coupe in perfect condition. All of this extra work is necessary when making a mold that must last during production runs.

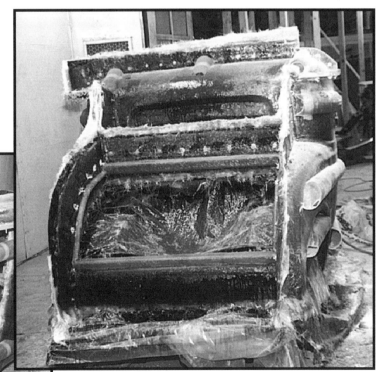

Excess flange material is trimmed away, to reduce the weight of the mold and to make it easier to rotate during body lay-up.

Beneath this heavy layer of fiberglass is a hot rod body and chassis, often the very best way to start any kind of body project, whether for production or one-off.

The mold has been removed from the plug, then it is inspected very carefully for any tiny imperfections (which must be repaired before continuing, should they exist). All of the flanges are in place, but parting agent is between each flange to ensure it will come apart when the body is cured.

The doors and deck lid are not integral with the body, they are molded separately. This has become almost standard practice in the industry, except in the case of special racing bodies. After the mold is buffed and waxed and any reassembly done, it is ready to be sprayed with production gel coat.

The mold has been gel coated with sandable gray gel coat and the first layer of fiberglass is started. The body is rotated during lay-up so that most panels receiving fiberglass and resin will be flat as the process continues.

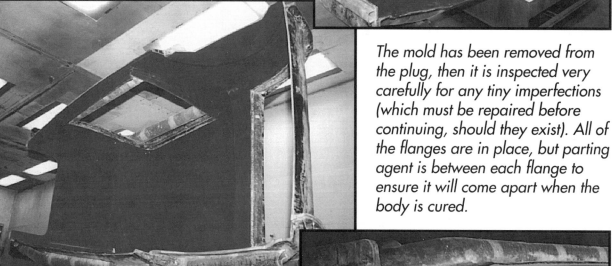

After the body has cured in the mold, the separation flanges are unbolted and the mold begins to come off. This is usually a one-piece-after-the-other procedure.

The reason to have flanges and a mold made in sections is that a typical body or complex fiberglass part will have curves that do not allow a mold to release easily.

The mold is handled carefully during assembly and disassembly to make sure the inner surfaces are not damaged.

Mike Slawson, left, and Bob Vollmerhausen own Class Glass, so they are intimate with all the steps needed to create a special body. Sometimes a mold needs extra persuasion to pop loose from a recently cured body, a rubber hammer or pry bar prove useful.

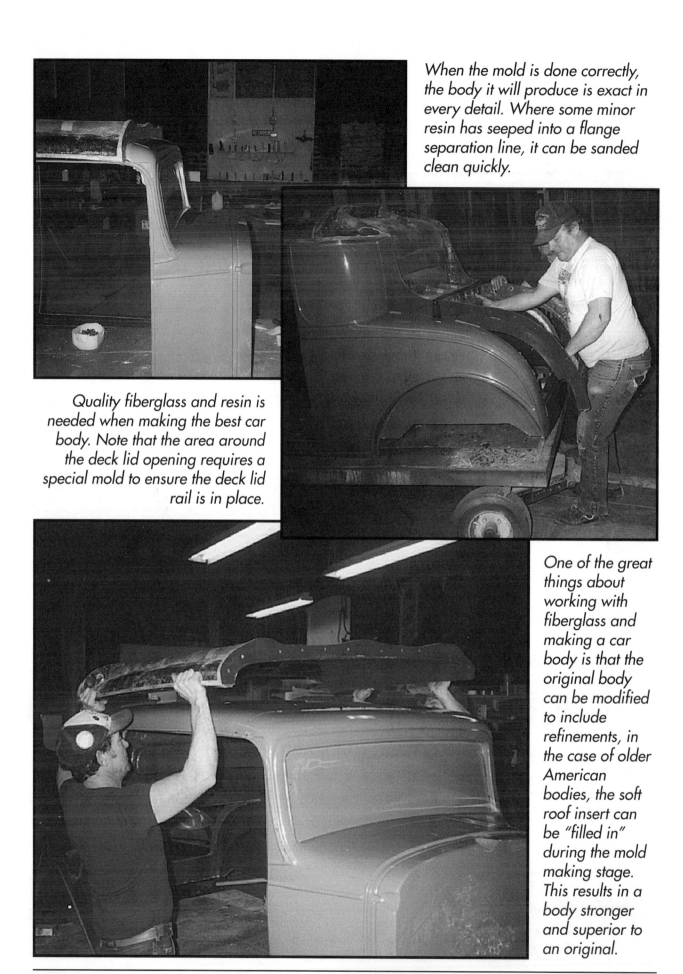

When the mold is done correctly, the body it will produce is exact in every detail. Where some minor resin has seeped into a flange separation line, it can be sanded clean quickly.

Quality fiberglass and resin is needed when making the best car body. Note that the area around the deck lid opening requires a special mold to ensure the deck lid rail is in place.

One of the great things about working with fiberglass and making a car body is that the original body can be modified to include refinements, in the case of older American bodies, the soft roof insert can be "filled in" during the mold making stage. This results in a body stronger and superior to an original.

Although nothing additional is needed to this production body, because it is fiberglass more modifications could be made easier than on a steel body.

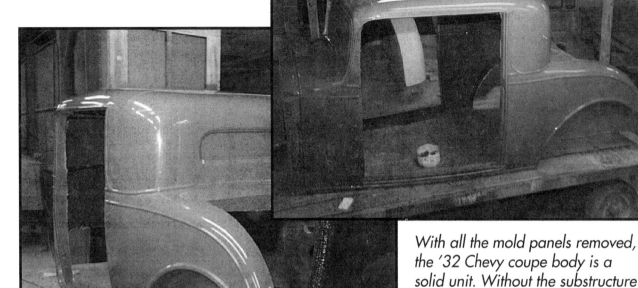

With all the mold panels removed, the '32 Chevy coupe body is a solid unit. Without the substructure installed, the body is still flexible.

Mike and Bob show off the completed 1932 three-window Chevy body, with all doors, deck lid, grille shell and fenders in place. A steel-reinforced floor has been installed along with wood substructure for hidden hinges and latches. All this is mounted on a specially built Martz street rod chassis.

FLATLANDERS HOT RODS

During the early 1970s, Alan Thornton answered requests from friends to help build hot rods, which led to opening a rod shop at home. In turn, this led to the decision that so many skilled craftsmen must face… get into business, or get out. Alan stayed in, for good, and Flatlanders began in 1978. At first, production centered on supplying parts from other manufacturers, but in 1985 it was decided to create special chassis. All this time, the inventory of available parts grew to include a full line of 1928-48 Ford bodies / chassis / components. In turn, this meant more attention to bodies, so that Flatlanders eventually purchased American Hot Rods and started fiberglass body production in earnest.

As with many hot rod body builders, Alan emphasizes that the Flatlander '32 Ford roadster and coupe bodies are "not kit cars," a reference to the reputation established by some sports style body / chassis combinations. Flatlander bodies are designed to fit stock Ford frames, and Flatlander chassis are designed to accept applicable Ford steel or fiberglass bodies.

Molds are made extra heavy duty for extended production lifetime. Each body is hand laminated, it takes two or three workers all day to lay-up the first layer of one and one-half-ounce cloth and two layers of Cormat, (This Cormat is used in the body only, fenders are regular production.) To avoid problems that can arise when 'glass is too thick in a body, the Cormat has proven very strong and easier to work with. All reinforcement for the body is via a steel skeleton. This is used to hold all the latches and hinges, and it does not touch the body in critical areas of interference.

The bodies are not marked or drilled for installation on a given chassis, since most chassis makers have different mounting points. Door and deck lid mounting points are drilled for mounting hinges. The customer does not need to add any reinforcement, this is already in place under the cowl, for the steering column, seat belts, etc. Bear claw door latches and window regulators are in place, as well as steel safety intrusion plates in the doors.

Alan Thornton stands amid fiberglass bodies at the Flatlanders shop in Norfolk, Virginia. Because the demand for chopped three-window Ford coupes has been so high, Alan tries to keep production a few units ahead.

A great deal of money and effort goes into making a fiberglass body mold. Anytime moving a mold is necessary lots of extra attention goes into transportation safety. Note the fiberglass tubes on the mold panels to add rigidity.

The Flatlander coupe can have any number of firewall variations. If the car is to be channeled over the frame this should be determined before the body is made so provision for a floor alteration can be included.

Steel tubing is used as the reinforcement skeleton for the bodies, this includes a place for the hidden hinges on deck lid to mount.

Most fiberglass bodies are made to accept original parts, such as the pivot pins on early Ford deck lids. Current design includes hidden hinges for these body parts.

There are some differences in body panels in the Ford line, this deck lid inner panel fits the five-window coupe and roadster. Note the metal reinforcing strips along edges of the panel, as well as the metal plates where the hinges will eventually bolt in place. This inner panel will be jointed to the outer skin to create an extremely strong completed deck lid.

A steel intrusion bar in a fiberglass door is a safety feature that does double duty as a mounting point for a window regulator in the coupe body.

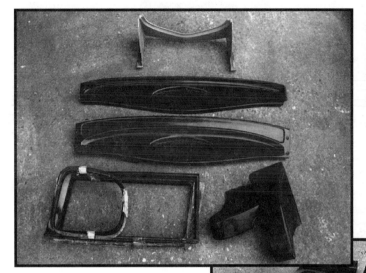

In addition to bodies, Flatlander produces fiberglass trim items, including the five-window Ford coupe door garnish molding at lower left.

Fiberglass fenders are popular with a wide buying audience, even owners of steel cars who cannot find steel fenders. For exact duplicates of originals, fiberglass fenders are a good choice.

OLD CHICAGO CHEVY

Another example of the non-traditional fiberglass body manufacturer would be Old Chicago Chevrolet, out of Clackamas, Oregon. Several years ago, the company decided to produce the 1934 Chevrolet body style, in three-window coupe style as well as roadster and cabriolet. More recently, they introduced a

The chopped three-window Chevy coupe from Old Chicago is becoming widely recognized in street rodding circles, in overall dimensions these bodies are similar to the Ford but with slightly more streamlined lines.

phaeton version that is getting lots of attention from serious builders.

The bodies are all hand laid fiberglass with extra strength and reinforcements to maintain maximum lifetime. Adjustable hidden door hinges mount to a tubing steel substructure, and steel is also used for coupe roof bows. The doors have a full steel inner skeleton with bear claw latches, the coupes have Specialty Power window mechanisms installed as an option. A unique design of tubing steel and 16-gauge steel sheet makes up the flooring, and the body skeleton runs from the cowl to the trunk area.

Fenders and grille shells are part of the accessory line for these cars, a style that is a strong match for the more common Ford.

The steel tubing substructure in Old Chicago bodies is larger than normal, giving rise to more strength in the mounted body. As delivered, the finish is a shiny black gel coat ready for finish prep and paint.

Because of the need for variety that produced the Chevy bodies meant a Chevy chassis was necessary, Old Chicago produces one. The frame is fully boxed for torsional rigidity, tubing crossmembers increase the strength. A Mustang independent front suspension is used, along with a four-bar rear end location and adjustable coil-over shocks. Many buyers of fiberglass bodies choose a chassis from the same company when such an item is available.

GIBBON REPRODUCTIONS

BY JOHN LEE

Approaching fiberglass car building from the viewpoint of a master auto bodyman is what Dwight Bond attributes to the success of his business, Gibbon Fiberglass Reproductions in Gibbon, Nebraska.

When Dwight had his own shop specializing in metal-finished restorations, "I was always concerned with fit and straightness," he said. He continues the same meticulousness with his fiberglass parts. His first 'glass products—Model A Ford roadster doors—were built to replace irreparable originals on restored steel bodies, so they had to fit and look right.

He started giving his Model A customers a price break for the privilege of making a mold from a component after he had returned it to perfect straightness. Within a few years Dwight had molded enough parts that it was just one more step to put together an entire body.

Now, as then, Gibbon bodies are built as individual parts and assembled, much as the originals were. Dwight explains that there are certain stress points, such as the corners of a deck lid opening,

As the automotive hobby expanded interest into the larger "fat fendered" cars, the Gibbon factory responded with two products that gained instant popularity. These two 1937 Ford cabriolets are examples of what can be done in fiberglass. The darker car on the left is a Club Cabriolet with seating for five, the white Cabriolet has a single inside and a rumble seat for passengers.

Both of the 1937s feature a two-and three-quarter-inch top chop and removable fiberglass tops covered in material to resemble true fold-down lids.

The 1937 Club Cabriolet has a regular opening deck lid, with a small seat behind the front seat for an occasional passenger or two.

where cracks develop due to body flexing, and fiberglass bodies flex more than steel ones. Reinforcing the bodies with wood as the originals were and bolting the components together leaves joints to relieve the stress.

Gibbon now makes plugs from perfectly restored cars, most of them Dwight's personal property. The plugs are then refined for better-than-original fit, or modified (a top chopped and filled, for example) and the production mold made from that.

Dwight and his crew also build and drive at least one example of each product so they learn first hand of any problems that need corrections before the body is released to the public. And since they've had the experience, they're better prepared to give helpful advice when a customer calls seeking help.

Gibbon started marketing such components as top inserts for Ford coupes and sedans, and a back door to convert a Ford tudor to a sedan delivery. Then there came a Model A roadster pickup with a removable C-cab roof. The business really took off with the 1933-34 Ford line; a roadster, phaeton, three-window coupe, and tudor sedan were available just when street rodding interest was shifting from the Model A and 1932 styles.

The 1933-34 Ford roadster was one of Gibbon's most popular styles and it still sells very well. John Barker built this one into a resto-rod in the late 1970s, it will fool many restorers until given the "magnet" test.

As shipped to the buyer, a 1933-34 roadster body comes in gel coat with a substructure in wood. Gibbon assembles the bodies differently than most manufacturers.

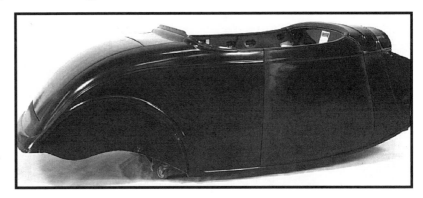

Dwight Bond is only average height, yet he towers over his V8-60 powered 1937 Model Y English Ford coupe. This body style was never built in Great Britain.

This is the regular-sized American 1933-34 Ford three-window coupe. This is one of the most popular coupes for chopping ever to swell a hot rodder's heart.

As fat-fendered Fords became attractive, Gibbon was waiting with a 1937 Ford Club Cabriolet, a runaway best-seller, followed by the 1937 and 1939 convertible coupes with rumble seats. The company was one of the industry's first to mold fiberglass top shells, which, when covered with convertible top material outside and upholstered inside, make open cars as cozy as coupes.

Trying to anticipate the market, which he's been quite successful at, Dwight built street rodding's first "compact" when the OPEC oil embargo hit. Though the 1937 English-size Ford

Bond installed nerf bar bumpers and rear fenders with Corvette taillights from an old custom coupe on his fiberglass 1939 Ford convertible.

The Gibbon's 1939 Ford convertible comes with a rumble seat, making this one of the more unique fiberglass bodies available to the general public.

Model Y (with shrunken U.S. 1934 styling) never caught on big, the coupe or sedan still makes a fun car for four-cylinder, V6, or nostalgic flathead V8-60 power.

Recent additions to the Gibbon line include some models passed over previously, notably the 1932 Ford "graffiti" five-window coupe, hiboy roadster, tudor, and Cabriolet. There's also a new 1932 Ford roadster pickup, a model that Ford built only a few copies of. A Model A sedan delivery conversion kit is also in the works.

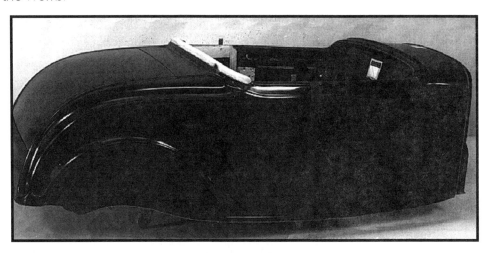

The Deuce roadster continues as one of the most famous of all specialty cars, the Gibbon version includes a wood substructure, full panel doors, and an upholstery rib behind the seat for correct era seat rolls.

Oval slotted mag wheels and hairpin radius rods spot this as a nostalgia hot rod, as do the original hinges and outside door handles, yet this is a new fiberglass body in gray primer.

The 1932 Ford three-window coupe has been replicated by several fiberglass suppliers, the original steel bodies used considerable wood in this design to gain strength. So does Gibbon.

Dwight says he has a personal interest in everything he builds, and his interests reach beyond the hot rod. The popularity of the mid-Fifties Ford pickups led him to develop a line of F-100 products, such as a glass top panel that allows chopping the 1956 top two inches without cutting the wrap-around windshield. There are also fenders, runningboards and rolled pans. His son Keith drives Gibbon's 1949 Mercury "test mule" to college. It has been used to develop no-rust quarter panels and a cowl, windshield and doors to convert a common coupe or four door sedan into an uncommon convertible.

Much as he loves Ford hot rods and

The 1933-34 Ford Tudor body easily outpaces the Fordor in hot rodder acceptance, this one comes already chopped for the serious builder.

This is one of Bond's earliest products, a sedan delivery conversion for a 1932 Ford sedan body. It is still available.

Merc customs, Dwight always thought the 1934 Packard convertible coupe was the epitome of elegance. So, he bought a restored one, made molds, and now markets a complete fiberglass car, any part of which will fit on an original Packard. Gibbon even tooled up to build repro frames to use late model torsion bar suspension and the builder's choice of V8 engine and transmission. That done, it was a small jump to build a 1934 Packard limousine with many of the same components. Dwight and Shelia's daughter and son-in-law operate a limousine service with the first one completed.

The 1934 Packard convertible coupe is recognized around the world as a premier classic, yet this outstanding example is entirely of fiberglass.

The '34 Packard convert spawned a Packard limousine, which in turned spawned a family spin-off business.

Keith Bond built a grille for a 1949 Mercury convert using five chromed F-1 Ford pickup truck grille teeth bolted to a custom fiberglass floating grille bar, that bar is now available for the custom market.

Finally, Dwight Bond with his very own roadster ride.

**The Only Company Devoted Exclusively
To Manufacturing Power Window Kits For Older Vehicles**

P & J Hot Rod Products

S ometimes, the very best manufacturers of specialty automotive projects labor in relative obscurity. Such has been the case of P&J out of Danville, Virginia. Well-removed from the major centers of automotive magazine media, the company had been doing its homework well and seemed to explode on the custom scene overnight with a radical chopped Mercury body. But in the background were a host of other fiberglass projects, as well as some specially built chassis. The word is out.

The astute spy would pick this out as a fiberglass mold, but it is for one of the new generation of "big" car bodies. The mold must include a tremendous amount of bracing, it is mounted on a rotating stand so the mold can be turned during the fiberglass lay-up.

When working with larger bodies, it is necessary to make the most of the opening parts as separate units. These are hand laid in individual molds and require considerable extra fitting.

Interestingly, the P&J chopped Mercury custom body does not require a mold of many different sections bolted together. If this were to be a drag racing body, the fiberglass laminate would be thinner (much weaker) and all opening panels would be molded as one piece.

The fiberglass Mercury body can be mounted on virtually any chassis with a similar wheelbase.

The Mercury body includes a large hat section beneath the doors, for strength. These complete bodies turn out to be less costly than a steel original after all the customizing is done. The top chop alone takes care of that.

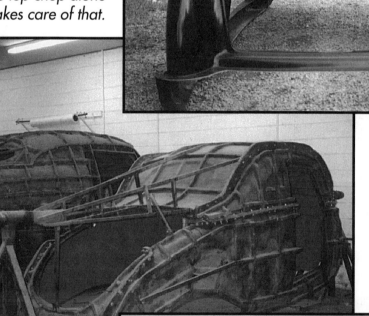

Almost overlooked in the rush to see the Merc custom is the 1940 Ford Deluxe coupe. This mold has a number of flanged panels making up the mold, thanks to the intricate shape of the body.

The '40 coupe body can be rotated on stands to get the mold at the best angle for laying the fiberglass and resin. This is a production advantage that the homebuilder of fiberglass bodies should consider.

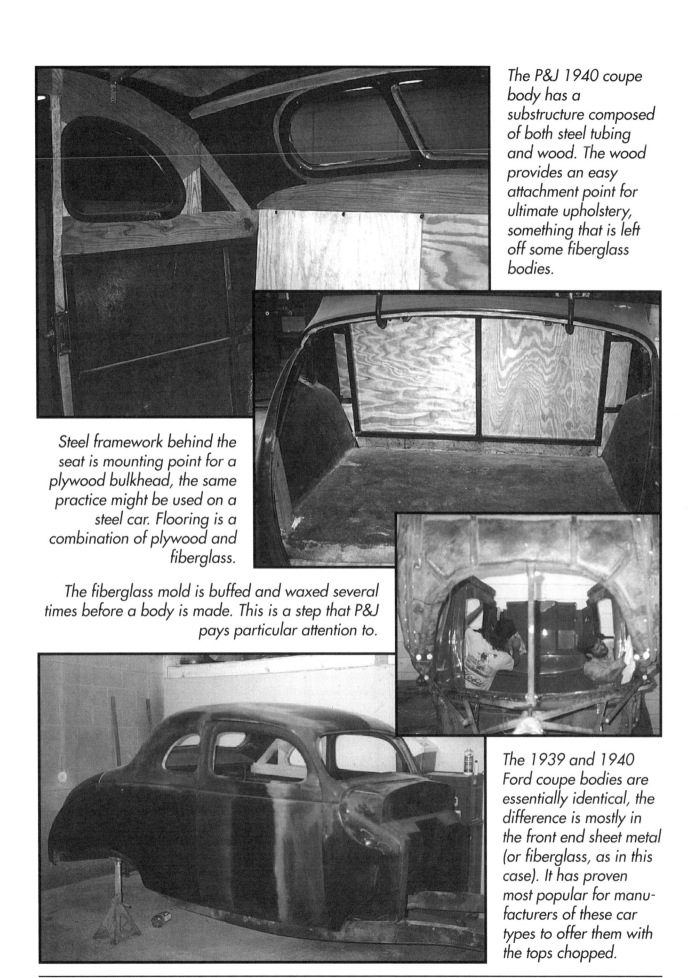

The P&J 1940 coupe body has a substructure composed of both steel tubing and wood. The wood provides an easy attachment point for ultimate upholstery, something that is left off some fiberglass bodies.

Steel framework behind the seat is mounting point for a plywood bulkhead, the same practice might be used on a steel car. Flooring is a combination of plywood and fiberglass.

The fiberglass mold is buffed and waxed several times before a body is made. This is a step that P&J pays particular attention to.

The 1939 and 1940 Ford coupe bodies are essentially identical, the difference is mostly in the front end sheet metal (or fiberglass, as in this case). It has proven most popular for manufacturers of these car types to offer them with the tops chopped.

An interesting trend at street rod runs in recent times has been the appearance of "fat fender" cars running without fenders! When the car is very low, the look is definitely that of a dry lakes racer.

Another major trend is running full-fendered cars dragging the ground.

This is how the P&J 1940 Ford coupe looks finished. It is about as low as possible, the proportions are very good with the chopped top.

Not as well known is the 1933-34 Ford three-window coupe. It is made same as the big cars.

The 1932 Ford three-window coupe is also chopped.

WINFIELD ROD & CUSTOM

The name Gene Winfield is second nature to every hot rod and custom car enthusiast of the past five decades, and no wonder. Gene started working out of central California in 1946, surrounded by some of the greatest builders of racers, customs, classics, and anything mobile known to man. He cut his teeth building metal creations, he learned aluminum crafting as a necessary adjunct to the trade, and he became a premiere fiberglass builder in the 1960s, when he moved to Southern California and the movie / TV shows needed special projects. Now, he has applied that knowledge to his own line of custom "big car" bodies, the most famous being a chopped Mercury. His specialties are fiberglass

The Winfield custom Mercury body is built in a mold similar to many, but it does have several flanged areas for underdraft. It is molded minus the floor.

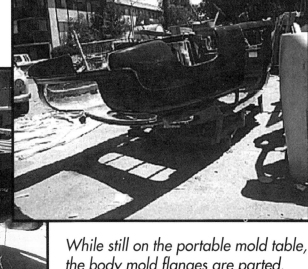

While still on the portable mold table, the body mold flanges are parted. The flooring is installed before any of the mold is taken apart.

Minor trimming is done as the mold flanges are removed, final finish is done after a careful inspection of the total body.

With the flooring in place, the body is lifted from the mold. This will take several people, as a big body is not lightweight.

replacement parts and complete bodies for Ford, Mercury, and Chevrolet. His business is located in Canoga Park, California. We asked him about his approach to fiberglass body building.

Winfield's products are thicker than most on the market, and he fabricates unique custom parts that are not available elsewhere. He uses metal for his substructure. Those frameworks last longer without the mold changing so much. This substructure is attached with epoxy, and is not entirely encased in fiberglass, which allows room for "breathing." When wood or metal is used to brace molds, the braces must be suspended off the molds before laminating to the back side. This can be done with foam or clay as a spacer. If this is not done, the braces telegraph through to the finished surface and that will show in every part made from that particular mold.

Winfield's bucks are made from wood, metal, and / or FRP foam. The wood and foam ones are used one-time only. Sometimes FRP plugs are used. The bucks are finished with plastic filler, then primed and painted with urethane or catalyzed enamel. The bucks are

Once the flooring (and in this case the package tray behind the rear seat area) is installed, the body gains a huge amount of rigidity. Still, it is handled with care to avoid scratches and tears.

then color sanded and rubbed.

Molds are made from fiberglass. Winfield uses tooling gel coat, then many layers of fiberglass that are hand laid, keeping each layer slow and cold. Separating flanges or multi-piece molds are made to get parts out of molds that are intricate and / or have an underdraft.

The number of times molds and bucks are used before replacement depends on several different factors. Sometimes with quickie molds (quarter-inch thick), he is able to produce 25 to 35 parts before replacement. Production molds that are one-half to three-quarters inch thick usually yield 100-200 parts, depending on the shape and configuration of the part. Of course, when Winfield talks production, he still means hand lay-up, not a factory procedure.

When doing a fiberglass lay-up, the Winfield crew begins by precutting the fiberglass matte or cloth to the size needed, which can be done while the gel coat is curing. The gel coat cures for one hour minimum. Gene points out that the gel coat is applied using either a brush or spray, and that it must be 25 to 30 mils thick, and must be catalyzed with the exact amount of catalyst recommended by the manufacturer! If the gel coat is too thin, the hardener in the resin might attack the gel coat on the first lay-up and produce a wrinkled (alligator) surface. If the gel coat is too thick, it makes the part too heavy and the part will be brittle in that area.

After the gel coat dries, a coat of catalyzed resin is applied. Then one layer of matte is applied. Before applying, the matte must be saturated (wet out). This is done by applying more resin over the top, which is then rolled out with rollers or brushed out. If making small parts, Winfield often wets out the pieces of matte on a cardboard surface. This allows him to turn the matte over easily, so he can

Gene Winfield sets the Mercury door in place on the raw body. All the parting lines and opening edges will be trimmed and sanded smooth before assembly and finishing. This particular body has a radical top chop with the slanted door posts.

On a large body, extra panels must fit well. For the Winfield Merc a stock hood and deck lid will bolt on when corners are rounded to match the fiberglass.

Flush-fitting glass is all the rage in every form of vehicle body today. The Mercury is molded to receive a flush-mounted windshield and rear window glass.

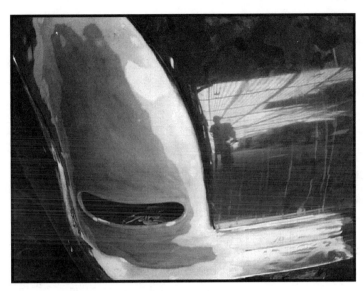

It is very easy to modify a fiberglass body for custom touches such as frenched taillights, this is something even the most amateur builder can accomplish.

wet the other side. The matte may then be picked up and applied in the mold. When the 'glass pieces are smaller, they are easier to handle.

When applying 'glass cloth to the make the part stronger, the cloth should be applied just after the matte has been wet out. By using this method, the cloth surface can be smoothed out. This gives a nicer looking job, and the part will be fairly smooth and uniform on the back side.

If more thickness is desired, in some places the crew might apply two layers of matte and one layer of cloth. Some fabricators use a sandwich lay-up, which is one layer of cloth, one of matte, and one of cloth. This isn't all that common anymore, at least in Gene's shop, as he found that when putting cloth on the gel coat, the cloth impression telegraphed through the gel coat. This impression is hard to get rid of (sanding, priming, and painting), which is why the matte seems to work better. Since there are different thicknesses in matte and cloth, samples are often done first to achieve the desired thickness on a finished project. No advanced composites are used at the present time, only polyester resins and hand lay-up.

All Winfield products are cured in the mold, for a minimum of 30 hours and usually 48 to 60 hours. It takes about 12 days to totally cure polyester resin. The longer the part stays in the mold, the better, with respect to having parts distort after they are removed. When Gene does a full Mercury body, it stays in the mold for two to three weeks. Segments are joined in the mold whenever possible. Door jambs, door posts, steel reinforcements, etc, are all applied to the body while it is in the mold.

Most Winfield fiberglass is ready to use when completed. On the Mercury body, the doors are fitted, hinged, and latched. The trunk is also fitted and hinged. However, some holes may need to be drilled. Seams from the parting lines of the mold are sanded, filled, and primed. Some stock parts will fit. On the Merc body, for instance, a stock steel hood will fit if the front corners are rounded. Same for the trunk, if the top corners are rounded.

No reinforcement to a delivered body is needed. The Mercury body, for example, will bolt directly to a stock chassis. Steel supports are needed to

Winfield makes a line of custom taillight lenses, for several different body styles.

channel the body over a later model chassis, a practice coming on strong of late. Door latches are included with a fiberglass body, and window regulators are an option.

Customers are advised to wash all gel-coated fiberglass parts with a strong detergent soap, then let the part dry. The surface is then block sanded with 80-grit sandpaper to remove slight imperfections. The surface should be primed with any good fast-fill primer. The primer should then be guide-coated and sanded with finer papers until the required smoothness is achieved. The part is then ready for paint.

Although the bodies and parts are all made of polyester resin and fiberglass, some epoxy fillers, catalyzed primers and catalyzed or urethane primers are used.

Once bolted to a chassis, the fiberglass Winfield Mercury is ready for transportation. Because the body can be channeled over any late model chassis with the right dimensions, it is easy to get very low to the ground.

WESCOTT AUTO RESTYLING

BY GARY MEDLEY

I f there is one name in the fiberglass industry to be forever interwoven into automotive history, it is that of Wescott. Dee Wescott started producing Model A fiberglass parts in the early 1950s, out of his automotive body repair shop in Boring, Oregon. Eventually, most of the family became involved in the growing business, now son Carl concentrates on the engineering while Dee continues to do product development. It is an effective combination.

Dee has been a life-long fan of all car racing forms, so it has also been natural that his knowledge and talents with composites would bring contemporary race car builders to his doors. Still, he

Because Wescott makes so many fiberglass bodies and parts, it is essential the company keep all molds in top condition. Storage is in clean areas away from lamination procedures.

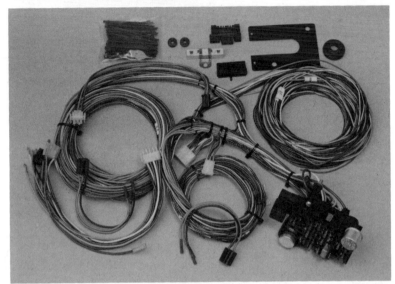

To get the most rigid mold possible, a frame of large metal tubing is made well outside the mold's outer surfaces.

is continually looking for ways to supply the seemingly insatiable hot rod and custom car market with products that are leading-edge in technology and safety. At the same time, Carl interspaces engineering refinements with face-too-face customer encounters at major hot rod activities around north America. "We find it very useful to show our product in person to potential customers," points out the younger Wescott. "On a rule, it will be three to five years from the time a customer first considers and looks at a fiberglass body until the purchase is made. Of course, professional builders are much more timely in buying. But the idea is that we get out to see what the hobby needs, and that the hobby has first-hand contact with us." With many hot rod events drawing over 100,000 spectators, this is a good sales philosophy. With either Dee or Carl, or

Molds are made to be rotated, either on a central pivot point or on the mold supports. This allows the panels to be flat for lay-up. All lamination is done by a crew of workers in an area devoted just to fiberglass and resin, this keeps the rest of the facility clear.

Wescott uses random strand matte in a hand lay-up process rather than 'glass cloth for the initial layer, it is felt this eliminates the problems of weave pattern bleed through to the part surface.

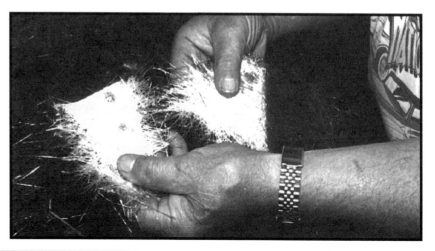

Multiple layers of 1.5 ounce matte are used in all Wescott operations, this allows the best possible wet-out of the resin and maximum strength. Small sections of glass are laid up at a time.

both, available to answer questions, an interested potential customer gains confidence in fiberglass as a viable automotive construction product.

Dee has been in the area (east of Portland) all his life. "I like it here," he says." We've grown the business slowly and steadily. Through ups and down in the general business climate, we've made it a point to never work on credit. We decide on a product, do our homework very carefully, then produce the best product possible. We try to estimate the demand, then we produce enough bodies or parts to stay ahead of the orders. That way there is little or no waiting for delivery, very important for us since so many of our customers are professional turnkey car builders. It just isn't the bodies or fenders that take our attention, either, since we often have to make up special hardware. In fact, Carl went back to school just to learn all the new developments in casting techniques so we could do some special windshield hinges for the '32 Ford three-window coupe. That's the kind of thing that goes on constantly. Keeps our attention, it does." To say that Dee and Carl Wescott know the fiberglass business inside out would be a gross understatement.

Wescott bodies and fenders are made from the same material, 1.5 ounce fiberglass matte cloth with a random structure. Note that this is a similar process to many other producers, and is getting away from the original method of starting with a 'glass cloth. The resin used is an isothalic polyester with a high heat distortion point of 190 degrees. Before 'glass is laid in the mold, a black gel coat is applied. This is a sanding gel coat with fillers, it is designed to be sanded and painted.

The fiberglass matte is made from random bits of glass strands, not a cloth weave. If the cloth weave is used, the weave pattern will often show through. As an example, early 1950s Corvettes were hand-laid with

A deck lid mold is prepared for production by cleaning thoroughly, then waxing and buffing the mold surface several times. No imperfection in the mold is permitted.

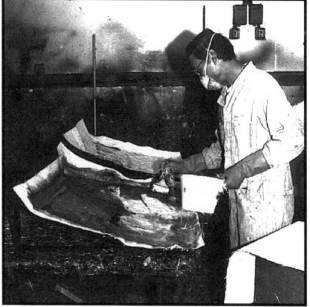

After a gel coat is applied to the mold, it is allowed to cure, then resin is applied and a layer of matte fiberglass positioned.

The fiberglass is thoroughly wetted out with polyester resin, air bubbles are worked out of each layer. Note the rubber gloves, full coveralls, and breathing mask on the worker.

glass cloth. Today, Corvette restorers who strive for authenticity use the same cloth, so the cloth pattern is imprinted on the car's final exterior finish.

The fiberglass matte Wescott has available is in different weights. But rather than using a heavier matte, Wescott uses multiple layers of the 1.5 ounce, which makes it easier to wet out with resin. Often Wescott will put two layers of matte down wet and then apply the third layer dry; it absorbs the resin from previous layers. The optimum resin-to-fiber ratio that Wescott likes is 60 percent resin to 40 percent fiber.

The foundation of fiberglass resin is styrene-based plastic. The fiberglass itself is just that, glass, as inert as a glass window pane. Styrene can cause a narcotic effect in concentrated levels. OHSA has set the safety standard in the fiberglass work place at 55 parts per million (ppm) for an eight hour day over a 40 hour work week. At 100ppm, you'll feel a little funny. At 200, you'll develop a craving for loud rock 'n' roll by Nirvana. Obviously, work should be done in a well-ventilated

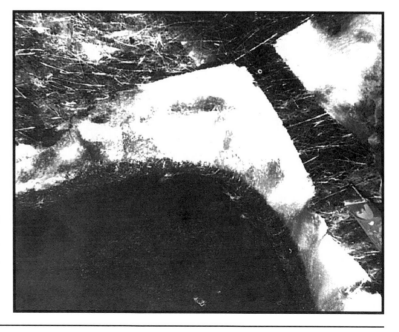

Fiberglass is lapped over the edge of mold, extra care is taken to ensure thorough wetting with resin around the edges.

Often, Wescott follows the first two wet layers of fiberglass with a single dry layer, this tends to soak up excess resin. Hand work removes any other extra resin. The overlapping fiberglass / resin can be trimmed just after the resin starts to kick.

area. Wescott has a complex arrangement of fans and air vents to keep shop styrene levels to an acceptable level. Workers also wear gloves, as styrene is absorbed through the skin. Dee points out that it isn't a good idea to put your head in the resin bucket, either.

Styrene can be detected by the nose at a mere .5ppm. Fifty ppm smells pretty strong, but is safe. For home projects, Dee recommends using a respirator with an organic vapor canister, similar to what painters employ.

After a part has cured in the mold, final edge finish is done with a grinder.

Safety also must be considered when grinding on fiberglass components. Fiberglass dust is a nuisance. If it gets on the skin, and is rubbed in, it will cause abrasions and itching. It is still glass particles. Cotton or paper overalls are recommended, plastic or vinyl protective gear will develop static electricity that will draw the particles. Wear a dust mask and safety goggles when grinding, contact lens wearers, be extra wary!

Although Wescott originally used wood extensively as a substructure, the company changed earlier on to steel. The biggest difference is that metal doesn't change with humidity and wood does. This means that when wood absorbs moisture it swells and pushes the fiberglass away from it. Then when it drys, the wood pulls away from the fiberglass. Also, metal is stronger than wood for safety considerations. There is so much metal structure in a Wescott body that their 1932 roadster body weighs 10 pounds more than the Ford original.

Wescott builds safety into the bodies by employing a metal substructure that supports the

Dee Wescott is considered by many to be the fiberglass car pioneer, he is still at it. The new 1932 Ford three-window coupe body gets windshield area flash trimmed away. The firewall and floor have been glued in place.

fiberglass panels. Included in this design are hefty side-impact protection beams. Wescott met with Federal DOT officials, who strongly recommended such protective beams, as well as securely and correctly positioned seat belt anchors.

So far, the feds haven't required crash testing of specialty cars, but Wescott suspects the next law to affect the sport will be mandatory air bags.

At the Wescott factory, the buck, or the original pattern from which the mold is made is typically an original new old stock part. Dee has, however, used some of his own fiberglass parts for bucks. When a buck is being made from a NOS item, it is fitted to the car and then braces are welded up and 'glassed in place to keep it from moving. The buck is then removed and finished until perfect. The buck is waxed to make it impervious to solvents from the mold making process. Finally, the mold is laid up over the waxed and well-braced buck.

When a mold is formed, one layer of 'glass is applied, wet with resin, and allowed to cure. Next it is sanded, before the additional layer of 'glass is applied, and the process repeats until seven layers are applied. Molds this strong can't distort, creep, or move in any way. The steel cage for a mold traps it for continued rigidity. Mold resins are made from two

This metal framework for a coupe door has provisions for hinges, latches, and a window regulator, the large corrugated beam is for crash protection. All metal parts are jigged and then welded so that each piece is identical.

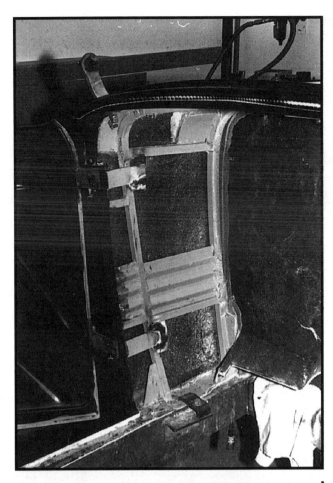

The metal substructure under a 1932 Ford roadster dash includes the same side intrusion bar as the door, metal support does not touch the fiberglass panels where it might imprint.

materials, depending on the applications: epoxy-based resins (which need less release agents, but are highly toxic) and vinyl ester resins.

On simple fender molds, such as a Model A Ford, up to 1,000 parts can be made in a mold before replacement. A typical body mold is good for 300 to 400 pulls. Wescott manufactures about three cars per week, about 125 a year. About 100 fenders are made each week, or about 5,000 per year.

Once the mold is completed, it is ready to start making parts. First, a black gel coat is sprayed on the mold, Wescott puts this on 15 to 20 mils thick. Once it cures to a tacky surface, the lay-up process begins. Each layer of 1.5 ounce matte is hand applied and wetted. Three layers are used for most parts. Once all the matte and resin is applied and air pockets smoothed out, the part is allowed to cure overnight. The resin combination that Wescott uses has a 20- to 25-minute cure time, if poured in an open container.

The metal frame substructures are bonded to the 'glass by two types of glues: A thick, pudding-like substance made from vinyl ester or a thinner methyl acrylic, which is the same stuff GM uses to glue together plastic minivans.

For a roadster door, an outer door panel is affixed to a rigid jig. The metal frame is positioned inside the panel and glued in place. Next, the inner door panel is set in place (everything still in the jig), and the combination is glued together. Strong, safe, and dead accurate. For the body framework, bodies are attached to a solid platform and the metal structure glued in place, using clamps. Whether body or door,

A roadster substructure is made out of metal. This makes a fiber-glass car body very rigid.

the metal frame is never attached to the inside of an exposed body panel, which would allow the metal frame to be "photo printed" onto the panel, visible from the outside.

It is emphasized that all the "extra" panels fit on Wescott bodies, each time and every time. The doors fit, the deck lids fit, etc. Dee advises that everything on the fiberglass car needs to be fit as a unit during final assembly. If one element is misaligned, that causes problems everywhere else.

Fiberglass and resin does shrink a bit during curing. This only affects right angle edges / corners, Dee says. To accommodate this shrinkage, he will modify the mold, making the angle more than the 90 degrees which will allow the part to shrink back to 90 degrees. As for general shrinkage, Wescott feels that if the resin is totally cured the shrinkage is negligible. Sometimes, however, if a part is incorrectly laid up and has thick and thin sections, waves can develop on long, flat panels. You see this on motorhomes.

When a fiberglass part doesn't fit, it can't be bent. Fiberglass has to be cut and relaminated. To this end Wescott keeps close tabs on whose aftermarket items fit best with Wescott fiberglass, such as metal grilles, etc.

Wescott produces up to 5,000 fenders a year, along with similar numbers of running boards and complementary pieces.

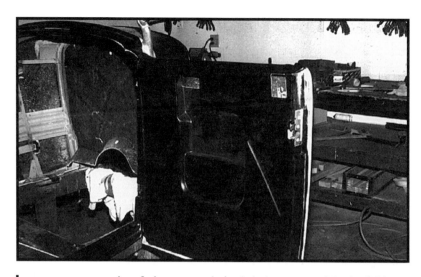

Interior panels of doors and deck lids are molded of fiberglass. The metal substructure is glued between inner and outer panels, the result is a door more rigid than steel.

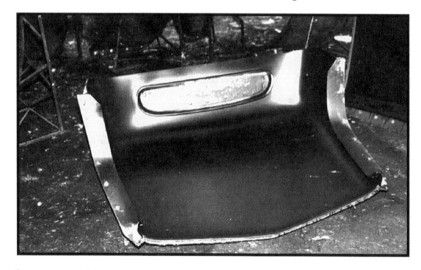

Special fiberglass tops can be made for roadsters, this gives coupe protection for the open cars.

One of the first bodies that Dee Wescott produced was for a Model A. The design is back with the metal substructure and updates such as hidden hinges.

Bodies are produced in numbers so that orders can be filled quickly.

The 1927 Model T roadster body has long been a staple of the hot rod hobby, Wescott has the style available.

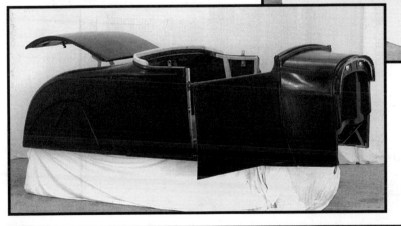

The 1928-29 Ford roadster body can include such modern items as hidden hinges and at the same time include wood for upholstery attachment. These bodies are popular with class racers as well as street rod builders.

The 1933-34 Ford roadster, with or without fenders, continues as one of the most commonly built fiberglass street rods. It is large enough to be comfortable yet small enough to not be considered a "fat fender" car.

The 1939 and 1940 Ford bodies are definitely "fat fender" size, yet they reproduce in fiberglass very well. This one includes fiberglass teardrop fender skirts to show off its custom potential. Quite a large number of these cars are being built around the United States.

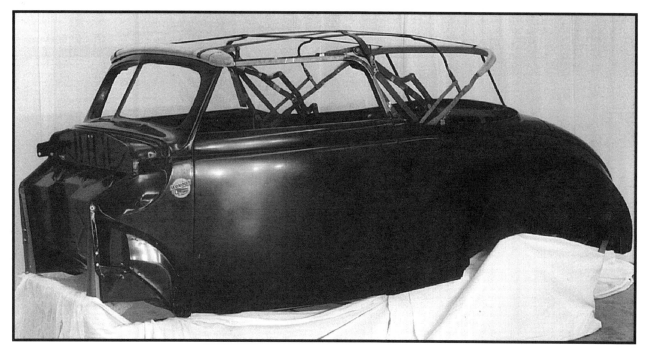

Dee Wescott was concerned that the late Ford convertibles have working top bows, even on the chopped top versions, so he engineered the entire bow system to fit his bodies. Both "long" and "short" versions are available for single and double seat bodies.

WORKING SMART

Poli-Form is another name that has become synonymous with premiere and innovative products in automotive fiberglass. Company founder Dick Williams has been an active hot rod and race car builder / driver since his teen years. He began working with fiberglass in 1948, as a hobby. At that time, the "wonder material" was all the rage for special car bodies, and he was repairing and restoring cars and boats. By 1970, the demands were so strong that he opened a business for manufacturing. Its current address is 783 San Andreas Road, La Selva Beach, CA 95076.

Although Poli-Form manufactures many products that have little or no connection to the automotive hobby, it is in the creation of special hot rod bodies and related components that the company has become known wherever such cars are built. Products range from Model T bodies (the 1915 version has a separate turtle deck, a plus for hardcore nostalgia builders, along with a 1919 Speedster body) through the popular 1929 Model A, to parts for

Dick Williams of Poli-Form demonstrates the strength of a fiberglass Model T Ford fender. It is not uncommon for a fiberglass part to be stronger than an original steel item, Williams makes his parts thicker for long street life.

Molds for fenders and other parts take up considerable storage space, but this is what helps keep a mold usable for several years.

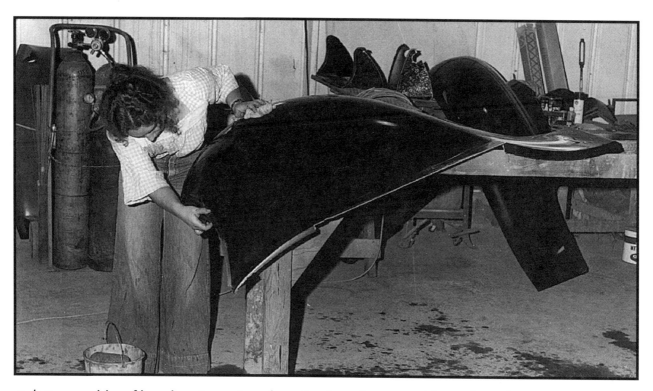

Poli-Form adds a fiberglass "rope" on front fender edges as additional reinforcement, the edges are trimmed before shipping.

Fords 1906-1957 and Chevy 1929-1936. This parts line ranges from fenders to running boards, gravel shields, splash pans, grille shells, fuel tank covers, dashboards, adapter aprons, wheel wells and deck lids. There are even parts for Porsche 924 and 911. Although licensed by Ford Motor Company to include the Ford logo on products, Dick has not used the logo to date.

Reflecting Dick's active participation in racing, all bodies are available in race "trim," such as the 1929 roadster with a tonneau for top speed runs as used in Bonneville, the drags, etc.

But the Poli-Form body getting intense interest from hot rod builders is the 1933-34 Ford three-window coupe. Recently, Williams checked on the first of these coupe bodies produced. That particular body was put through some rather

Careful inspection will spot small imperfections, it takes very little additional preparation to use fiberglass parts.

Keeping an inventory of popular fenders and other parts is necessary to supply the growing number of car builders who are selecting fiberglass materials.

rigorous testing at the plant, including a couple of 20-foot drops (no damage or stress noted). During the ensuing years, the car has been on the road almost constantly, the only damage has

been to door hinges when the owner inadvertently opened a door at speed. This body uses a welded steel cage-type reinforcement that includes a shoulder harness mount and steel intrusion bars in the doors. Wherever anything is installed, such as doors and deck lid, the attachment is directly to the steel

With the advent of new "old style" hot rod chassis and a full compliment of bodies, accessory items such as gas tanks were a natural. In the case of the 1932 Ford, it is easiest to make a steel tank and add a fiberglass tank cover that duplicates the original. This is the female mold for such a cover.

It is possible to use available fiberglass parts to assemble a complete car, perhaps more so for hot rods and sports cars than for customs, at least for now.

reinforcement. As with several upscale fiberglass body builders, Poli-Form includes everything needed to assemble the body. Door hinges are forged steel with hardened pins, hidden hinges are an option, window moldings are included, and window regulators are installed. A full dash is included, as well as upholstery tack strips. In short, the body is ready to bolt in place and finish for paint.

Poli-Form recommends taking the time to do all the fitting correctly. If the body is to be run without fenders, most of the fitting is moot. But, if fenders and other attendant parts are to be used, fit the parts to the body / chassis before doing any drilling, sanding, or finishing. Start with the running boards, which are bolted to the frame, but loosely so the boards can be shifted slightly for fit. Clamp the rear fender to the running boards, then check for alignment. Remove the fender and drill mounting holes slightly

Poli-Form has been a major supplier of incidental panels for older body styles, including running boards and splash aprons.

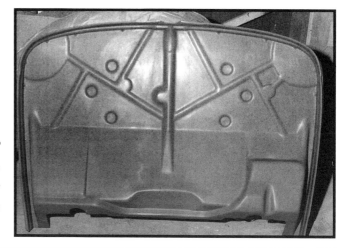

The Poli-Form firewall is available as an exact duplicate of the original Ford item, or a recessed unit is made that provides engine clearance.

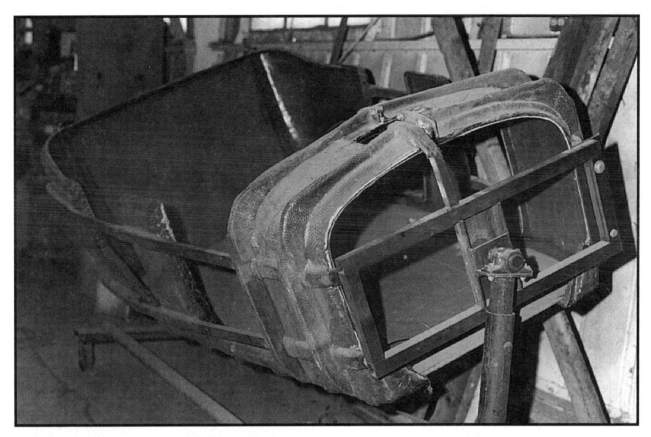

The Model T touring body mold is mounted on a pivoting framework so the body can be laid up in the most convenient position.

larger than the mounting bolts (so the fender can be shifted for alignment). Poli-Form molds the fender lip slightly long where it bolts to the running board, after everything is fit, the extra lip can be trimmed to match the board. Use regular large outer diameter fender washers between the bolt heads / nuts and the fiberglass, and do not overtighten the bolts (which would damage any fiberglass). Fit the front fenders—on the '34, this will take extra patience. Do not try to distort the fenders to fit braces, make the braces fit the fiberglass. By bolting everything together loosely, and shifting the parts during assembly, a good final fit is possible.

For the finish, Poli-Form advises sanding the fiberglass with 220-grit or a higher coarse sandpaper. Smooth and round rough edges with 80 grit, followed with 180 grit. Prime with a catalyzed primer, or a lacquer primer. Remember that the lacquer takes two or more weeks to cure. Wet sand with 320-grit sandpaper for the enamels, 400- to 600-grit for lacquer.

A stock, oval-opening Ford dashboard.

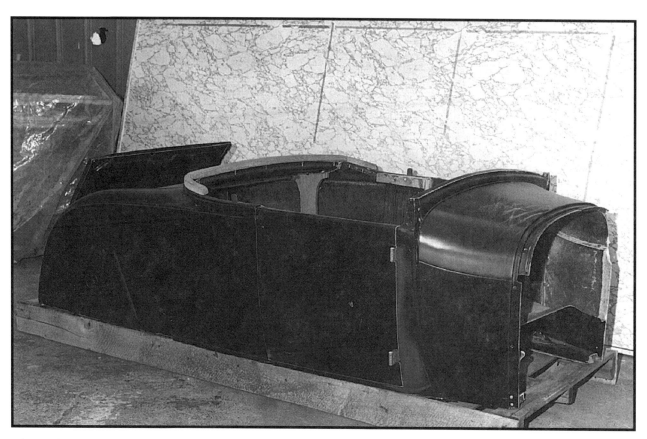

The Poli-Form 1929 Ford roadster features a three-piece cowl section that includes the original seam. This body is also available in a competition format.

Williams includes chassis and other parts that a fiberglass body buyer may need to finish a project. Poli-Form bodies come ready to bolt to the frame.

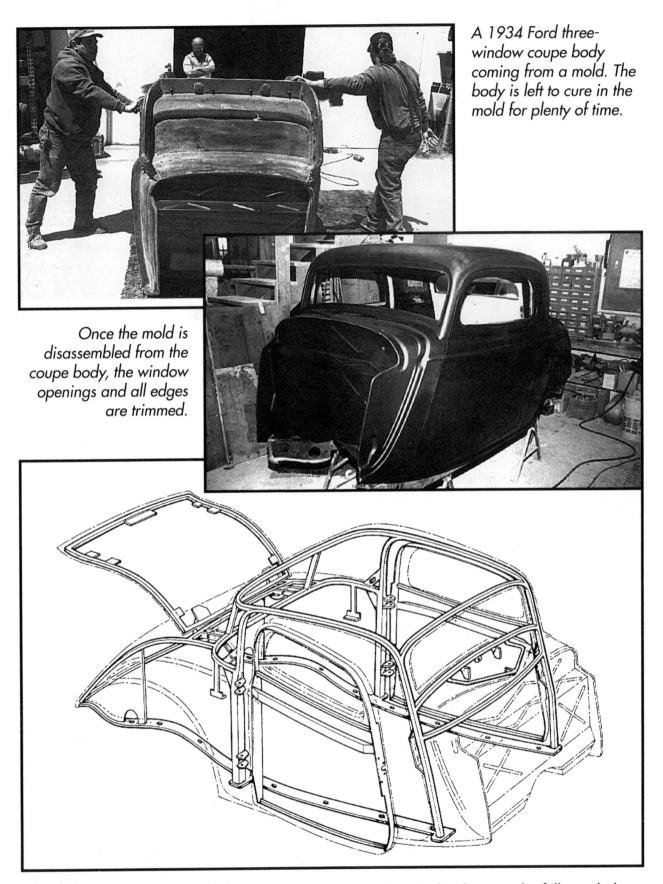

A 1934 Ford three-window coupe body coming from a mold. The body is left to cure in the mold for plenty of time.

Once the mold is disassembled from the coupe body, the window openings and all edges are trimmed.

The Poli-Form metal substructure includes steel intrusion bars in the doors and a full metal plate along the floor base where the body bolts to the frame.

Although a full metal substructure is glued to the body for reinforcement, considerable wood is added for the package tray and roll-up rear window mechanism.

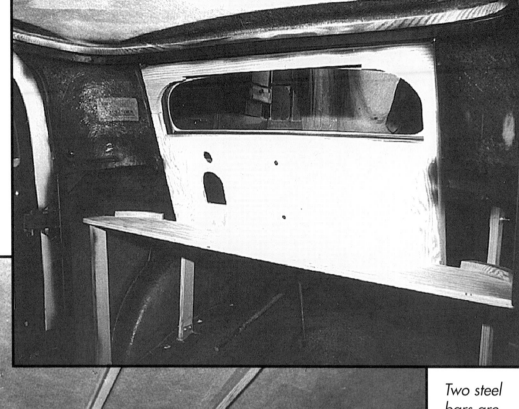

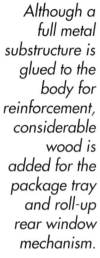

Two steel bars are used under the top for additional strength and as a safety feature.

The original Ford-style plunger latch is replaced by a modern bear claw unit, which holds much better and is especially apropos on a front-opening door.

The '34 coupe door is an inner and outer shell glued together around the steel frame, the finish is exceptional.

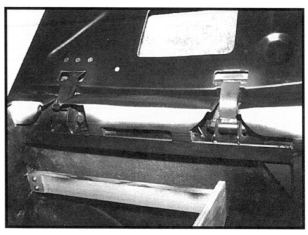

Whether regular exposed or more modern hidden door hinges are used, they mount directly to a steel frame at the door post.

An operational cowl vent is available, most builders leave this item blank in favor of under-dash air conditioning units.

Williams shows off his own 1927 Model T track roadster. Dick makes the nose piece and the unusual three-piece hood from fiberglass. A customer can order anything, from a single piece to all the components needed to assemble a rolling car.

HARWOOD INDUSTRIES

Gary Harwood has been a specialty car enthusiast since his teens and a drag racer almost as long. His efforts in the plastics / composites industry go back to the late 1960s, when he was working on his own race cars and hot rods. His hobby grew from the home garage to a part-time small warehouse, into the huge supplier it is today. Harwood's name has come to be associated with a vast array of unique fiberglass products used on racing cars, with 35,000 fiberglass parts sold annually. From his shop in Tyler, Texas comes everything from 1955 Chevy bodies to racing fuel cells to a new honeycomb composite 1932 Ford street roadster body, which we feature here. If it has to do with cars, and with fiberglass, you can bet Harwood knows about it.

One of the spin-offs of heavy competition in the hot rod body field is a huge variety of offerings, and as with the Harwood '32 Ford roadster body, lots of improvements to make the finished car more user-friendly.

Although Harwood has a heavy back-

Note the super fit of the door and the high reflective quality of the body. Harwood does not use any wood or metal substructure in the body, instead the fiberglass and composites are designed to add strength, as in the flanges and steps added to the rear fender well area. Harwood makes hidden hinges that extend into the door for maximum adjustments in all directions, and the doors open 90 degrees with built-in stops. The latches are rotary safety design. The door opening A-pillar is a complete channel molded integral

Many fiberglass body suppliers are paying particular attention to finish of the panels, this particular body style responds well to modern paint techniques.

with the cowl and floor, and the dash is bolted in. The interior door sill has been reshaped with compound radius front and rear to minimize wind noise and water intrusion.

ground in both ends of the business (as a user and a producer), each new product must undergo review and approval by a company committee. This determines what the product is intended for and how it will be made. The decisions on fit-finish-appearance, however, are automatic: They must be premium.

All Harwood production molds are made with special tooling gel coats and fiberglass procedures developed over many years of experience. The molds are made in-house, and all are reinforced with composites. Extreme care is used to eliminate any heat sink properties that would

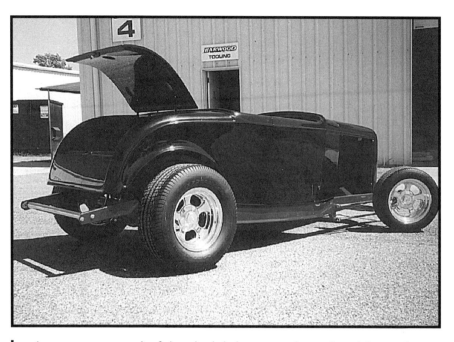

The interior panel of the deck lid is smooth, with additional composite reinforcements added. Inner flanges have been redesigned for more efficient sealing and water run-off control. Inner corners have compound radii to eliminate the body cracking commonly found in this area. The hidden hinges are fully adjustable. The deck lid latch area has a double reverse molded full length bottom sill flange for extra strength and a place for the latch receiver.

The rear of the '32 body is flush so that any stock or aftermarket gas tank will fit the original style frame; a rolled pan is optional. The bottom of the body is smooth, and the rear area has been raised and reshaped to accommodate contemporary suspension and exhaust systems.

The honeycomb composite reinforced body has a cockpit area lengthened two inches at the seat back area, in turn the doors are two inches longer for easier entry. The firewall is recessed for engine clearance and contoured for engine heat bleed-off. The compound double channel firewall perimeter gives maximum cowl rigidity and strength. In addition to the new roadster, Harwood is working on a 1932 three-window coupe and a 1932 sedan delivery.

telegraph through the mold because of the chemical heat values induced (thermodynamics). The mold support structure is carefully engineered to eliminate mold sag or deformation due to the actual weight of the mold. Bucks are made in a variety of ways, from using an original part to constructing a graph table and making a buck from clay.

From the beginning of a project the likely number of parts needed from a given mold is calculated, this determines the type and quality of the buck / mold to be produced. Currently, Harwood has nearly 2,000 molds in service.

Because of the quantity involved, Harwood prefers a strict production line technique. The company believes this is the only way to control consistent quality and continuity when large numbers are involved. Even so, they also insist that all products be created by hand lay-up, and different products may require different materials and procedures.

The company reports spending tens of thousands of dollars experimenting with different advanced composites. Some have worked, others have not. This on-going research and development is an extremely important part of the business.

A full line of accessories are available, including a billet aluminum grille for the fiberglass shell.

Not satisfied with torsional strength in available chassis for the '32 roadster, Harwood elected to create their own unit with nearly 70 feet of round tubing used to make the crossmember. Frame rails are available aftermarket items in .134-inch wall thickness.

Personnel regularly attend technical seminars around the country so they can stay educated on new fiberglass technology and fabrication techniques.

The new 1932 Ford roadster body is an example of this advanced technology: The fiberglass is reinforced with honeycomb composites for super strength and rigidity.

Once a part is placed in the mold, it is left there to cure. Harwood has found this a vital area in manufacturing. Gel coats, buffering agents (to eliminate print-through), cloth / matte formulas, resins (which they formulate in-house), catalyst formulas and percentages, heat and humidity, all play a very big part in the successful lamination process. Segments are joined in the mold, to ensure product integrity fit and finish while eliminating surface distortion from curing adhesives.

Harwood prefers to use neither wood

A double driveshaft loop is built into the crossmember. The transmission mount is well forward for trans removal without disturbing the engine.

Knee-Deep in Knuckle Scraping!

That's what HOT ROD MECHANIX is all about. CSK Publishing has teamed up with Tex Smith, one of the founding daddies of hot rod publishing, to bring you the baddest, best, tech-hip hot rod book around. As well it should be—Tex's been chopping his teeth on hot rods since the '50s! HOT ROD MECHANIX will be loaded with how-to's and what-for's for fat-fendered fanatics, lead sled heads and custom-crazies.

So jump on the bandwagon today! We'll send you a year's worth (six issues) of HOT ROD MECHANIX for only $15.95, plus we'll throw your name in a hat to win a trip to Bonneville (Tex will love to meet you).

Send coupon to:
HOT ROD MECHANIX
P.O. Box 1010
Denville, NJ 07834

STEP BY STEP

CHOP THAT CONVERTIBLE TOP

TEX SMITH'S

HOT ROD MECHANIX

THE HOW-TO RODDER MAGAZINE

MAY 1994

OUTLAW '34s
Special Section:

Latest Craze! Fat Fendered Truckin'!

Top 10 Rodder Tools
Wiring Harness Buyer's Guide
Bonus Installation Tricks!

USA $3.25
CANADA $3.75

HOT ROD MECHANIX

For faster service, call 800-221-8700
(for credit card orders only)

Okay, sign me up!
❏ Here's my $15.95 for six issues of HOT ROD MECHANIX.
❏ Bill my ❏ Amex ❏ Visa ❏ MasterCard $15.95 for six issues of HOT ROD MECHANIX.

Card No._____ Exp. Date _____

Signature _____

Name _____

Address _____

City _____

State_____ Zip _____

Offer good in the U.S. only.
Canadian price: $23 (Canadian dollars, money orders only).

TSB

nor metal substructures, as the company believes both have negative points. Expansion and contraction, adhesive qualities, etc., seem detrimental to the quality of the final product. Instead, they prefer to engineer strength and rigidity through shape and radius contours, interior channels, and reinforcement with different composites such as honeycomb and carbon fiber. Their perspective is that nothing adheres to fiberglass like fiberglass.

Delivered products are ready to be installed. Doors hung and latched, deck lid hung and latched, windshield frame fit and installed—all this because they understand the engineering behind the products and they feel this gives complete customer satisfaction. Generally, most OEM-style items fit, unless Harwood has made design or engineering improvements. In this case, everything is carefully discussed with the user before hand. The customer is required to add no reinforcements. All standard body shop painting procedures apply.

Because so many rod builders want the car extremely low, the front or rear of the frame rails can be notched for spring / axle clearance.

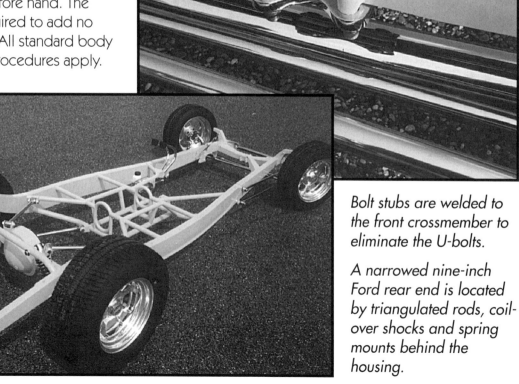

Bolt stubs are welded to the front crossmember to eliminate the U-bolts.

A narrowed nine-inch Ford rear end is located by triangulated rods, coil-over shocks and spring mounts behind the housing.

FIBERGLASS RACE CARS

Fiberglass has been popular for one-off car bodies since World War II, but it wasn't until the 1960s that it became widely accepted as race car material. Competition dune buggies led the way, followed by drag racing Funny Cars and stockers running fiberglass body parts. Composite innovation in the aerospace industry was quickly adopted by the sports car and high speed oval racing fraternity, with exotic materials used for everything from body pieces to chassis to suspension components. In some forms of racing, however, the disintegration factor of fiberglass and the exotics means that certain body parts are not allowed. Although body panel cost comparisons prove fiberglass and the exotics competitive with metals, mechanics like 'glass because it is easy to make replacements. It is also excellent for unique body styles and making changes "in the pits."

RON MAIN'S RECORD BREAKER

Ron Main built this car strictly to run for a single Bonneville Salt Flats record, a Lakester class with a speed of 165 mph. The engine was a highly modified Ford Flathead V8 (pre-1954 era) and the result made possible by engine power and this body was 190 mph! We have detailed the engine thoroughly in our companion book *The Complete Ford Flathead V8 Engine Manual,* the body we chronicle here.

Because of its aerodynamic shape and exposed wheels, this car is classified as a Lakester rather than a fully enclosed streamliner. The body consumed over 1,200 man hours of labor, built by Aerosmith of Southern California. The canopy took 200 man hours.

A perfectly flat table was built for the body buck, then body formers were cut from plywood at stations equidistant down the body length. These were secured to the table, and aligned with wooden stringers, same as building a stick and tissue model airplane fuselage. Although there are no perfectly flat areas on the body, the sides were close enough so that sheet material could be tacked to the buck as foundation for the later plaster.

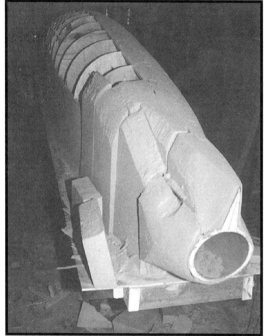

In body areas where there was considerable contour, foam blocks were attached to the buck formers. This foam was carved into shape and trimmed to get a foundation near the finished product.

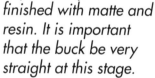

The entire body area can be covered with plaster, which sets nicely and can be shaped easily, or finished with matte and resin. It is important that the buck be very straight at this stage.

A great deal of time was spent sanding and filling and sanding some more to get the buck absolutely mirror smooth. As with any ground-up fiberglass building program, the finished product is only as good as the buck and mold.

SOURCES

WHERE TO GET FIBERGLASS BUILDING PRODUCTS AND COMPLETE BODIES

SUPPLIERS

The following are places where you can buy fiberglass materials and complete fiberglass products. This is not a complete inventory, that might be nearly impossible in an industry always in flux, still, many of these companies have been supplying materials for decades. Some are huge companies, while others are smaller, more specialized dealers. Nearly all have information available and telephone contacts willing to help you with a project. This will prove especially true of companies that sell in the aircraft industry, in which having the correct information about fiberglass usage has immense safety implications.

Some manufacturers will have rather extensive technical information about their products available, with detailed suggestions and instructions on use. Do not deviate from these manufacturer recommendations. All fiberglass products and all resins are not the same. Some products are made for mass marketing and are only marginally useful for building a car body or part. Other products are far too advanced (and expensive) for use on a car. Talk to several local suppliers to learn what you should buy. And remember that too many suppliers will have employees who know little or nothing about what they are selling! If you do your homework, you'll find that larger communities often have suppliers who furnish the trade. Sometimes these wholesalers will sell to you, or if you are buying in quantity, they may refer you to a dealer. But they almost always tell you exactly what you need, the trade names (which sometimes vary across the country), and special use tips that you'll find valuable.

Do not buy surplus fiberglass materials unless you are absolutely confident in the seller. The fiberglass itself can be contaminated with dust, oils, just about anything that will settle on an open package. Resin has a very definite shelf life, and so do fillers.

You may be able to buy a larger amount of fiberglass material and resin, as well as attendant tools and supplies, from a wholesaler. Figure about what you will need, buy in bulk, and later add any small amount you may have figured short. If you are going to do an entire body, you are going to spend a lot of money (which is one reason you may want to buy a commercial body, then make custom changes), so if you can save at the wholesaler that's a plus. If you get friendly with a fiberglass product manufacturer, that may be a source for savings (and building tips).

The point is, do your supplies (and suppliers) homework. In our listing of manufacturers of bodies and parts, it is often the case that a manufacturer makes cross-over products. The maker of an early Ford body may also make late model parts, for example. It is not often, however, that a manufacturer of classic or sports car-style bodies makes hot rod or race car products. Several manufacturers make component parts for nearly every type of car, and they generally advertise heavily in the magazines. In our listing, we put these companies where we see them most active. For the classics and sports car area, there is an organization titled Specialty Constructed Vehicle Association, 2111 Poinsettia, Long Beach, CA 90805; (310) 422-9167. The SCVA is an excellent starting place for information on these manufacturers.

It is imperative to shop around and get recommendations on body and parts suppliers. Because of a few unscrupulous marketers, especially in the sports kit car field, that end of the industry has received a black eye. The very best approach is to talk with buyers for opinions. The obvious problem with this is finding a buyer of X-product. You can find them at car shows, sometimes, and often if you air it around the car enthusiast circuit you'll get info on particular companies and products. It also works very well to contact assemblers, professionals who build fiberglass-bodied cars for customers (they advertise in kit car magazines). Read magazines on the subject—the street rod magazines for hot rods and customs, kit car magazines for the sports and classics. Above all, talk to car building enthusiasts. The underground telegraph works extremely quickly and efficiently in spotlighting shoddy merchandise and disreputable manufacturers. Any company unwilling to give references is possibly suspect.

Although a body kit may be advertised as complete, it is not always complete, as in "absolutely everything needed to assemble a car." Find out what you are getting, in writing, and get the actual delivered price, in writing. Telephone promises don't cut it. Never send the full purchase price unless you have absolute confidence in the company, a small initial payment is all that is usually required. Full payment can be due on delivery. Never accept a partial shipment of parts. Take the time to inventory what you have received via the trucking line, and note the condition. If a manufacturer is reputable, you will be contacted if there are any problems or delays in sending the order.

MATERIALS

Although much of the fiberglass materials introduced to the public several decades ago are still viable, change in this field continues. It accelerates as more and more uses for advanced technology are applied to the marketplace, an excellent example of this is the wide utilization of molded plastics in contemporary automobiles. Adhesives are replacing traditional fasteners to hold body panels; race cars have chassis of exotic fibers and resins; and plastics are even being experimented with inside engines. While much of these advances come from the aerospace industry, widespread applications are everywhere.

Some of these composites are boron fiber, carbon fiber, aramid fiber (which is Kevlar), and may include products of rayon or nylon. Unfortunately, they are expensive and not always as well-suited to a car body as the more mundane polyester resin combination. Also, note that many body manufacturers now use matte alone (sometimes now spelled mat), rather than the cloth / matte / roven sandwich. Much of this can be attributed to the use of the roller tool rather than a squeegee and to better fiberglass structure. The improved surface matte is a finish quality, structural matte may be the second laminate. The common "E" glass is what most homebuilders will be working with, but there is an "S" glass available. This is a structural glass with smaller fibers, it is stronger than "E" glass, and usually used with phenolic, epoxy, or vinylester resins.

The foam most commonly used for making a buck is a urethane sheet; it can be cut and sanded to shape. A spray or pour-on urethane is also available, which is sometimes much preferable to plaster. This foam has a soft surface, and it can be covered with a couple coats of polyester resin. After this cures, a layer of eight-ounce cloth and resin is applied to make a hard surface. Ordinary body filler and a lot of sanding is done to get a perfectly smooth buck. The materials supplier will also have a product called microballoons (glass bubbles). This can be mixed with laminating resin and fumed silica to be a great filler. All this replaces the plaster method.

The following is just a sampling of manufacturers of materials, your local supplier will have a more comprehensive listing. You can often get excellent reference information direct from the manufacturer.

ADHESIVES:

3M Corporation
Alexander Aeroplane Company
Ciba Composites (Ren Plastics)
Crest Products
Cytec
Dow Chemical
Hexcell
Hysol
Kwik Poly

CASTING RESINS:

Kwik Poly

RESINS:

3M Corporation
Alpha Corporation
Ashland Chemical
BASF Chemical
Ciba Composites (Ren Plastics)
Cytec
Dow Chemical
Hexcel
Kwik Poly
Owens Corning Fiberglass
Pacific Anchor Chemical
Shell Chemical

FIBERS:

Amoco Chemical
Atkins & Pearce
BASF Chemical
Burlington Glass
CertainTeed Corporation
E.I. DuPont (Kevlar)

FIBERS: (CONTINUED):

Hercules, Incorporated
Manville
Owens Corning Fiberglass
PPG Industries
Reade Advanced Materials

FOAM:

American Klegecell
Dow Chemical
Mobay Corporation

MICROBALLOONS:

3M Corporation

HONEYCOMB:

E.I. DuPont
Hexcell

ADDRESSES:

3M Corporation
St. Paul, MN 55144

Alexander Aeroplane Company
P.O. Box 909
Griffin, GA 30224

American Klegecell
204 North Dooly Street
Grapevine, TX 76051

Amoco Chemical
200 East Randolph Drive
Chicago, IL 60601

Ashland Chemical
P.O. Box 2219
Columbus, OH 43216

Burlington Glass
1345 Avenue of the Americas
New York, NY 10105

CertainTeed Corporation
P.O. Box 860
Valley Forge, PA 19482

Ciba Composites
515 East La Palma
Anaheim, CA 92807

Dow Chemical
P.O. Box 0994
Midland, MI 48686

DBSF Chemical
100 Cherry Hill Road
Parsippany, NJ 07054

E.I. DuPont
Kevlar Specialty Products
Center Road Bldg.
Wilmington, DE 19898

Hercules, Inc.
Hercules Plaza
Wilmington, DE 19894

Hexcell
11711 Dublin Blvd.
Dublin, CA 94568

Hysol
P.O. Box 312
Pittsburg, CA 94565

Kwik Poly
P.O. Box 1233
O'Fallon, MO 63366

Mobay Corporation
Mobay Road
Pittsburgh, PA 15205

Owens Corning Fiberglass
Fiberglass Tower
Toledo, OH 43659

PPG Industries
One PPG Place
Pittsburgh, PA 15272

Reade Advanced Materials
45 West River Road, Suite 228
Rumson, NJ 07760

Shell Chemical
1 Shell Plaza
Room 1673
Houston, TX 77002

CLASSIC & SPORTS BODIES / PARTS

A.C. Exotic Cars
12955 York Delta, Unit J
Cleveland, OH 44133
(Cobra)

Ace Auto Services
21422 Parthenia Avenue
Canoga Park, CA 91304
(Cobra)

American Fiberbodies
P.O. Box 726
Xenia, OH 45385
(Sports)

American Sports Car Design
324 Home Avenue
Maryville, TN 37801
(Mustangs)

Antique & Collectable Autos
35 Dole Street
Buffalo, NY 14210
(Classic / sports / hot rod bodies)

ASPP
1240 East Gilbert Drive, Unit 2
Tempe, AZ 85281
(Cobra / GT 40 MK II)

Auto Designs
2013 South 6th Street
Klamath Falls, OR 97601
(Rebody parts)

A-Z Emporium
5400 Griffin Road
Davie, FL 33314
(Fiero rebody)

Beck Development
1531 West 13th, Unit E
Upland, CA 91786
(Lister)

Blue Ray G.T. Engineering
416 Woodline Drive
The Woodlands, TX 77386
(Datsun rebody)

Cervini's Auto Designs
1234 N.W. Boulevard
Vineland, NJ 08360
(Mustangs)

C-F Enterprises
P.O. Box 1347
Long Beach, CA 90801
(Ace)

Classic Antique Replicar
10712 North May Avenue, Suite D
Oklahoma City, OK 73120
(Sports racer)

Classic Factory
1454 East Ninth Street
Pomona, CA 91766
(Auburn)

Classic Motor Carriages
16650 N.W. 27th Avenue
Miami, FL 33054
(Sports cars / hot rod bodies)

Component Craft
10728-E South Pipeline Road
Hurst, TX 76053
(Cobra)

Contemporary Classic
115 Hoyt Avenue
Mamaroneck, NY 10543
(Cobra)

D&D Corvette
534 Wingerter Street
Akron, OH 44314
(Corvette)

Erra Replica Automobiles
608 East Main
New Britain, CT 06051
(Cobra)

Euro-Works
3771 Eileen Road
Dayton, OH 45429
(Fiero rebody)

Everett-Morrison
5137 West Clifton Street
Tampa, FL 33634
(Cobra)

Exotic Enterprises
459 Madeline Avenue
Garfield, NJ 07026
(Sports car)

G.L. Cars & Concepts
3329 Term
Burton, MI 48529
(Fiero / Trans Am rebody)

Handcraft Motorcar Company
6805 Riverview Blvd.
Bradenton, FL 34209
(Camaro / Firebird)

Hardy Motors
P.O. Box 1302
Bonita, CA 91908
(Allard J2X)

Heritage Industries
1 Heritage Place
Frazee, MN 56544
(Classics)

Hi-Tech Motorsports
2204 West Southern Avenue
Tempe, AZ 85282
(Cobra)

I.C.M. Industries
901 South Greenwood, Unit A
Montebello, CA 90640
(Porsche speedster)

I.F.G.
1574 El Prado Road
Chino, CA 91710
(Countach)

Indy Exotics
7610 Lake Road
Indianapolis, IN 46217
(Cheetah)

Integrity Coach Werks
2802 S.E. Monroe Street
Stuart, FL 34997
(Cobra)

Johnex
18 Strathern Avenue
Bldg. A North, Unit 36
Brampton, Ontario
Canada L6T 4L8
(Cobra)

L.A. Exotics
6900 Knott Avenue, Unit E
Buena Park, CA 90621
(Cobra)

Lone Star Classics
715 Katy Road
Keller, TX 76248
(Cobra / Mercedes / Corvette)

Lucas Autodesign
P.O. Box 14052 , N.E. Plaza
Sarasota, FL 34278
(Camaro / Trans Am rebody)

Marple Automotive
300 North Main
Shelbyville, TN 37160
(Camaro / Firebird rebody)

Memory Motors
110 West Avenue G
Conroe, TX 77301
(Early Corvette)

Mid-America Industries
1519 East 1st Avenue
Milan, IL 61264
(Corvette)

MidStates Classic Cars
835 West Grant
Hooper, NE 68031
(Cobra)

PISA
P.O. Box 15088
Phoenix, AZ 85060
(Fiero rebodies)

Predator Performance
12280 - 75th Street North
Largo, FL 34643
(Jaguar)

**Prototype Research &
Development Ltd.**
230 Albert Lane, Box 1330
Campbellford, Ontario
Canada K0L 1L0
('57 Chevy / others)

Puckett Auto Works
12650 Highway 67
Lakeside, CA 92040
(P-250 GTO)

ReMarque
207 Side Street
Stayner, Ontario
Canada L0M 1S0
(Cobra)

Shell Valley Motors
Route 1, Box 69
Platte Center, NE 68653
(Cobra / parts)

S.M.C.
4656 Bridgewater
Fayetteville, AR 72703
(Cobra)

Spartan Motorcar Company
1655 South Rancho Santa Fe Road,
Suite 108
San Marcos, CA 92069
(Classic)

SSZ Motorcars
111 Zagato Lane
Aniwa, WI 54408
(Shark)

Sun Ray Products
8017 Ranchers Road
Minneapolis, MN 55432
(Bradley / parts)

T. Green
5621 East Bonna
Indianapolis, IN 46219
(Sports car / Cobra)

Trident Motor Group
1108 Solana Avenue
Winter Park, FL 32789
(Sports cars)

Unique Motorcars
230 East Broad Street
Gadsden, AL 35903
(Cobra)

Vintage Speedsters
12112 Centralia Road
Hawaiian Gardens, CA 90716
(Porsche speedsters)

Vortex Motorcars
P.O. Box 37
Vancouver, B.C.
Canada V5N 2S3
(Sports car)

VR Engineering
406-3K South Rockford Drive
Tempe, AZ 85281
(Sports car)

Warp Five
1500 N.E. Roanoke
Blue Springs, MO 64014
(Sports car)

Westfield Components
17 Knight Street
Watertown, CT 06795
(Lotus-type sports)

HOT ROD / CUSTOM / RACE BODIES & PARTS

The 34 Corner
5A Blackwater
Hurn Road, Christchurch
Dorset BH23 6AF, England
(Ford bodies)

Aeroglass Fabrications
Route 2, Box 2150
Nashville, GA 31639
(Chevy parts)

Ai Fiberglass
6599 Washington Blvd.
Elkridge, MD 21227
(Bodies / parts many makes)

A.J.'s
Route 3, Box 284A
Jersey Shore, PA 17740
(Off-Road)

Aero Fiberglass
3250 - 50th Street S.E.
Delano, MN 55328
(Trailers)

BeBop's Glass Works
1000 Tennessee Avenue
Etoway, TN 37331
(Ford bodies / trailers / pedal cars)

Bitchin Products
9392 Bond Avenue
El Cajon, CA 92021
(Steel firewalls / floors)

Carolina Custom
Route 3, Box 376
Clinton, NC 28328
(Ford / Chevy / Plymouth dashes)

CBI
13750 Mooresville Road
Athens, AL 35611
(Willys / Ford / Chevy bodies)

Champion Fiberglass
9471 Hemlock
Shreveport, LA 71118
(Trailers)

Class Glass & Performance
101 Winston Street
Cumberland, MD 21502
(Chevy bodies)

Coach & Chassis Works
1445-A Babcock Blvd.
Pittsburgh, PA 15209
(Dodge / Plymouth
 bodies / parts / trucks)

Dagel's Rod & Truck
1048 West Collins Avenue
Orange, CA 92667
('34 Ford mini roadster body)

Deuce Customs
23 / 12 Edina Road
Ferntree Gully, Victoria, Australia 3156
(Ford bodies)

Downs Manufacturing
715 North Main
Lawton, MI 49065
(Ford bodies / parts)

Fairlane Company
210 East Walker Street
St. Johns, MI 48879
(Ford bodies / parts / trucks)

Fiberfab International
16649 N.W. 28 Avenue
Opa Locka, FL 33054
(Ford bodies)

Fiberglass & Wood Company
Route 3, Box 1000
Nashville, GA 31639
(Chevy bodies / parts)

Flatlanders Hot Rods
1005 West 45th Street
Norfolk, VA 23508
(Ford bodies / parts)

Hastings
Rural Route 1, Box 625
Sesser, IL 62884
(Ford bodies)

Harwood Industries
17824 State Highway 31 East
Tyler, TX 75705
(Ford bodies / race parts)

Gibbon Fiberglass Reproduction
Box 490
Gibbon, NE 68840
(Ford / Packard
 bodies / parts / trucks)

GlassTek
105059 Schoger, Unit 40
Naperville, IL 60540
(Race car parts)

IDA, Inc.
RD 2, Box 331A
Morganville, NJ 07751
(Willys bodies / parts)

J&J Enterprises
2615 Jonquil Lane North
Plymouth, MN 55441
(Trailers)

Kentrol
P.O. Box 3734
Youngstown, OH 44513
(Off-Road)

Minotti's Fiberglass Products
1981 J & C Blvd.
Naples, FL 33942
(Ford bodies)

Motion Glass
598 Sunrise Highway
Baldwin, NY 11510
(Parts)

Old Chicago
16169 S.E. 106th Avenue
Clackamas, OR 97015
(Chevy bodies / parts)

Osborne Productions
Thorn Place
Napier, New Zealand
(Ford bodies)

Outlaw Performance
P.O. Box 550
Avonmore, PA 15618
(Ford / Chevy / Willys bodies / parts)

Oz Rods
Steve Upton
Shop 5
15 Mining Street
Bundamba, Ipswich, Queensland
Australia
(Ford bodies)

P&J Hot Rod Products
6262 Riverside Drive
Danville, VA 24541
(Ford / Mercury bodies)

Performance Fiberglass
109 West York Street
Biglerville, PA 17307
(Race car bodies)

Pete & Jake's
401 Legend Lane
Peculiar, MO 64078
(Ford bodies)

Ply-Do
Route 1, Box 277B
Delbarton, WV 25670
(Plymouth / Dodge bodies)

Poli-Form Industries
783 San Andreas Road
La Selva Beach, CA 95076
(Ford bodies / parts)

Progressive
401 West Lone Cactus Road, #3
Phoenix, AZ 85027
(Dash / door panels)

Race Composites
260 Lambert Street, Suite F
Oxnard, CA 93030
(Carbon fiber hoods)

Ravon
701 Daniel Street
Billings, MT 59101
(Ford bodies / parts)

Rods 'N Rails
2876 Apopka Blvd.
Apopka, FL 32703
(Ford bodies)

Romeere Products
33767 Groesbeck Highway
Fraser, MI 48026
(Trailers)

Ru Car Crafters
3637 South 177th Avenue
Sand Springs, OK 74063
(Trailers)

R.W. Johnson
3330-F Mary Lane
Auburn, CA 95602
(Trailers)

SAC Products
633 West Katella Avenue
Orange, CA 92667
(Kevlar Ford bodies)

Southeastern Fiberglass
P.O. Box 24070
Fort Lauderdale, FL 33307
(Ford bodies / parts)

Speedway Motors
P.O. Box 81906
Lincoln, NE 68501
(Ford bodies / parts / kit cars)

Sunrise Street Rods
P.O. Box 62
Laketon, IN 46943
('33 Plymouth body / parts)

Superior Glass Works
15721 South Windy City Road
Mulino, OR 97042
(Ford / Chevy bodies / parts / trailers)

Total Performance, Inc.
400 South Orchard
Wallingford, CT 06492
(Ford bodies / parts)

Unlimited Performance
560 West Rincon
Corona, CA 91720
(Parts)

U.S. Body Source
Star Route 1, Box 800
Hampton, FL 32044
(Off-Road)

VFN Fiberglass
501 Interstate Road
Addison, IL 60101
(Race car bodies / parts)

Wescotts Auto Restyling
19701 S.E. Highway 212
Boring, OR 97009
(Fords bodies / parts)

The Willy Works
Junction Routes 17 & 52
Liberty, NY 12574
(Willys bodies / parts)

Windsor Fabrications
850 West Goguac
Battle Creek, MI 49015
(Ford bodies / parts)

Winfield Customs
7256 Eton
Canoga Park, CA 91303
(Ford / Mercury custom bodies)

Yogi's
P.O. Box 68
Calamus, IA 52729
(1946-48 Ford convertible bodies)

Zipper Motors
504–28 1/2 Road
Grand Junction, CO 81501
(Ford bodies)